Hiking to Hell and Back!

Two Caminos de Santiago on Foot, 2007–11.
One Spanish pilgrimage tripled from Italy.
One 7–11, *not* a store of convenience!

Michael Keane

A Pilgrim of St. Jim

Uno Peregrino de Santiago

Author of
A Voice in the Wilderness,
a 3,000 mile amble over more than mountains,
and *A Pilgrim's Progress—Possibly*, a complete circuit
of Ireland, every foot on foot, and more...

HIKING TO HELL AND BACK

MICHAEL KEANE, PILGRIM OF ST. JIM

Epic Press

Belleville, Ontario, Canada

ISBN: 978-1-55452-887-5
LSI Edition: 978-1-55452-888-2
E-book ISBN: 978-1-55452-889-9

Cataloguing data available from Library and Archives Canada

To order additional copies, visit:
www.essencebookstore.com

Or please contact:
pilgrimofst.jim@gmail.com
P.O. Box 365, Waverly, NY 14892

Epic Press is an imprint of *Essence Publishing,* a Christian Book
Publisher dedicated to furthering the work of Christ through the written
word. For more information, contact:
20 Hanna Court, Belleville, Ontario, Canada K8P 5J2
Phone: 1-800-238-6376 • Fax: (613) 962-3055
Email: info@essence-publishing.com
Web site: www.essence-publishing.com

Printed in Canada
by

E*p*ic
*P*ress

This work is dedicated to:
One singular mom,
Two mates (Australian/Austrian),
and The Three Amigos

Contents

BOOK 1

On the Pilgrimage of St. James, el Camino de Santiago

Not a guide, this book merely recounts my own experience of pilgrimage. My advice? Go without a guide, explore for yourself, pick up advice as you go, though I'll try to include a few practical suggestions here. Let's start with buying good shoes and learning to tie them properly. After that, as long as you don't overdo and do rehydrate, you can't go far wrong just following the blessed/blasted yellow arrows all along the sacred route, pointing ever westward.

"Adelante! Por Dios y Santiago!"

CHAPTER 1

Ireland/France to Pamplona, Spain

8:00 a.m. 8 Oct. 07

It's a miracle! 7:00 a.m. surprised me still in bed, in a hostel in Bantry, Co. Cork, two long bus rides from Shannon Airport. The first bus (7 a.m. service to Cork City) doesn't even head the right direction. Luckily, the wristwatch of this ex-New Yorker runs ever fifteen minutes fast. Up and out, showered and shited, running half-dressed and half-packed, half-assed and half-baked at the bus stop, as a church bell tolled 7:00…I discovered my bus ran fifteen minutes late, of course.

That one-quarter hour could cost me dearly later. Connecting in Cork City for the airport in County Clare could end in a close call anyway. My missing a bus two days ago, because it left early, only augments my annoyance now. That misstep made for some hard hitching from Tralee, Co. Kerry, to Ardgroom, Co. Cork, where I'd last left off hiking completely around Ireland. The final stretch of that troublesome tour will need to wait till I return—unless I miss my plane…

3:00 p.m.

Now bound on a second pilgrimage, I'll supply details later. What you need to know now: I did make my non-refundable economy flight to Biarritz, France. Not only did traffic this morning allow me to catch the ever-punctual coach to Shannon Airport, it permitted me to bypass Shannon for Ennis, where luggage waited. Collecting and repacking my packs, I caught a bus back to the airport—just in time! I do confess to a little anxiety though, a lack of faith. Everything needed to jive just right today. Making my flight meant more fully laden running. Yet I'm really flying now, while sitting relaxed, albeit possibly with an ulcer. It is a miracle.

08/10/07; 9:30 p.m. French time

Ain't it funny, how luck runs hot and cold, like a faulty shower in a cheap hotel? Landing at Bordeaux-Biarritz Airport, I felt unsettled by that feeling inflicted whenever every sign reads in a foreign language. Of course, I'm the foreign material. So, I looked for help, and looked again. Finding the woman paid to help, I felt relieved—foolishly.

Had she done her job, told me which bus serves the official hostel, I would not have missed that bus and "missed the boat." I missed the first bus by seconds; waiting and wondering I missed the second bus by fluke. Parked too long, with all my luggage, I boarded the third bus without one essential item. "Stop, stop, *arrettez*!"

Off I pop, sprinting pell-mell to recover my hiking staff. Back aboard, I brokenly gasp the importance of the proper staff for a pilgrim of St. James, Iago, or Jacques. Possibly though, a stick ain't worth the €100. 00 ($150) that my mad bolt left lying between the bus stop and bus.

This bad start foreshadows evil for a poor pilgrim. Perhaps it's only fair for a pilgrim of such little faith. I had felt fate turning against me. Walking around Ireland, I had pushed luck too hard. Weary and dehydrated, I noted impaired memory and decision-making and vowed to let up on the pedal in France. As soon as I could locate accommodation, I intended to rest. As the hostel sits out of the way, I might better have blown €100 on a hotel nearby, rather than leave the sum lying in the street. Yet, had the tourist info person just given correct info to the tourist, I'd have garnered a perfect day. Oh, "there is a tide" indeed.

11:00 a.m. Biarritz 09/10/07

Last night I thought myself lucky to find a hostel with fine facilities. I just missed dinner though, and all the shops closing. Arriving too late to do laundry too, I did it anyway. Staff shut down machines early because washer and dryer, taking interminably long, keep guests awake. Laundering sure kept one guest awake.

Once my troubled head hit the pillow, it would not rise until minutes after the breakfast service, when I learned their *petite dejeuner* worth waking for, even for a coeliac sufferer. More irritating, I find my left eye irritated for no known reason. Perhaps I'm allergic to peculiar pollen or, more likely, to bed-linen detergent. A crawling insect could be the culprit. A fly buzzes about the room now, but not for long...

If this throbbing eye turns worse, I'm up to the eyeballs in the stuff flies love, as I've no insurance or health plan here.

6:00 p.m. 09/10/07

A man can change the mind of Lady Luck. Just never try to push her. Today, I adopt a leisurely pace, a relaxed pose. My hostel stay extended, I report to police my *purse perdu*, but without expectation. En route, I pick up tourist info, purchase provisions, plus a train ticket, and return to the hostel, before re-emerging to hunt for more groceries—all done in an orderly, unhurried fashion. Never did I flee the scene of my great misfortune (a lucky spot for someone). I will depart calmly tomorrow, grateful not to have lost more.

Possibly too relaxed, I've missed by minutes the open hours of two supermarkets. *Supermarchés* come few and far between here and close early. But, I'm not bothered. Hungry and excluded does *not* feel as bad as losing €100.

My ma taught me to pray to St. Anthony for any item lost. One calm moment does often bring success to a desperate search. More appropriate in this case, calling on St. Jude, patron of hopeless cases, might help. Possibly St. James would better serve a *peregrino de Santiago*. Alas, I have no faith in saints, dead or alive. So why, you ask, do I set out on a month-long pilgrimage?

I seek to maintain belief in myself. Something could salve the soul, in the here and now, if not save it in the hereafter. Having vowed to myself, on a sudden fancy, to walk through Spain from France, I will do the deed or die trying.

I'd like to restore my faith in humanity too. I am told this trek, though testing to an individual, enlists and rewards a communal effort. We'll see. Once I shared a family, a home, and a dream, only to find I really held nothing, nothing but the road. So, the road it is then.

Thank you, kind reader, for keeping me company.

- - - - -

Before going farther, let me complete the strange story of the lost wallet. What does it mean? You tell me.

Resigned to my loss, I returned today accidentally to the scene of the accident. Missing one bus, I took the only other available to another supermarket. Too late, finding the door locked, I tramped towards where I knew a bus would return. Flagging one before my wallet admitted to lacking right change, I entered the nearest shop but failed to acquire the required coins. Hence, I carried on in the direction of yesterday's fateful bus stop.

Yes, I admit to examining the sidewalk one more time before entering the next shop. Below the counter, I found more than change. The previous customer had left her purse. Gallantly, I sprinted after the damsel, her favor held above my head as Don Q would do. Not recognizing her own purse, the forgetful female thought me bold for bawling at her in the street. The shopkeeper had to come out to explain and receive thanks. You must admit the peculiarity of my losing a purse and then finding there (the very next day) someone else's purse for them.

10/10/07, 7:30 a.m.

Yes, I am up on time. Not only that, I'm showered and laundered before breakfast, not to mention dressed. Seems I'm too excited to sleep. My peepers popped open at 5:30. I attempted returning to dreamland, for my fellow dorm dwellers, though they would never appreciate my waiting an hour on my upper bunk. Instead of counting sheep, I mentally listed each item in my backpack and carry-on.

1 pack-cover	2 disposable razors
1 ground sheet/poncho	1 small soap bar
1 sleeping bag	1 mini shampoo bottle
10 pkts. tissues	1 small towel
1 toothbrush	1 small scissors
1 small toothpaste	1 French dictionary
1 sm. stick deodorant	3 pair socks

1 pair walking shoes	25 vitamin pills
1 pair plimsolls	5 T-shirts
2 notebooks	1 pants
1 jackknife	1 short pants
10 plastic spoons	6 undershorts
50 pc. Sugar-free gum	1 sweatshirt
In carry-on:	1 mini sewing kit
2 notebooks	1 mini first aid kit
1 newspaper	1 packet wet wipes
2 water bottles	6 maps
2 phones and chargers	1 sml. chess set
2 mini flashlights	1 card deck
asstd. personal papers	1 sudoku book

My belly pouch held all the real essentials: passports, tickets, currencies. My most necessary staff didn't fit.

The list below assumes my being fully dressed, including hiking boots, jacket and big hat. One pair of shorts, underwear, socks and plimsolls I carry in a carry-on, in case the pack gets lost. More socks and an umbrella need to be bought.

Packed last, one locker key keeps safe another big bundle of belongings. Yet I am still seriously over-packed, according to scuttlebutt. If disciples of the apostle truly travel as light as rumored, the mountain air must reek to high heaven. Maybe we're meant to offer up BO like incense. Santiago town should smell any pilgrim's approach. (P.S. Forget extra shoes and much more.)

Further rumor puts me on a hiding to hell, for nil and naught. The paths and hostels may already have closed for the season. For certain, the weather soured today. Rain falls intensively, a first for this trip (France or Ireland). As proof for the existence of God, consider the obvious cosmic sense of humor. Excuse me for not laughing. The joke's on me.

On the Train

See, I did make the train, despite the rain, and the need to make up this morning for missing breakfast yesterday. After a final futile check for my wallet, I failed to realize what else I'd left behind until after boarding the train. My passport went uncollected at the desk!

If taking passports from guests constitutes a stupid policy, not collecting one may seem more idiotic but isn't my policy. If all hostels and hotels collected passports, I would have a routine for their collection. Now, as the train powers towards an international border, I travel without passport. I refuse to turn back, though, before I'm turned back.

Maybe I should have checked into this trek more thoroughly beforehand, but feared spoiling spontaneity. Afraid of fostering preconceptions, or breeding forbidding misconceptions, I thought ignorance might set me free. Sure enough, here I am, but weighed down with too much gear in order to arrive ready for anything.

I presumed also that more accurate info would become available here. Another mistake. All I know now is the requirement to report to someone somewhere in St. Jean Pied de Port in the French Pyrenees for a pilgrim passport. Although many other recognized starting points exist for this legendary medieval pilgrimage, most routes converge on this village. After crossing the mountains and all of Spain, I expect to locate the tomb and shrine of St. James, apostle of Jesus, brother of John, patron of pilgrims and of Spain. The legend of his beheaded body being returned from Jerusalem to western Spain looks even less likely than my walking there. Thirty days I'm told that task requires. Three weeks will need to suffice. Yet I lack strength anymore for running under pack over mountains. The harder I push at the start, the less likely I'll finish in Santiago.

1:15 p.m., St. Jean

The Pyrenees appear suddenly to travelers by train. Terrain saying nothing of mountains disappears as your train enters a tunnel, and presto, you emerge in steep rocky gorges among odd domes and crazy crags. Strange beasts and hidden villages surprise the passing stranger more.

St. Jean, medieval walled market town, welcomes foreign hordes now. Surrounding mountains make walls almost superfluous. From here the peaks appear ominous to a hiker.

4:00 p.m.

Leaving the train, I overhear the stationmaster whistle a tune very like "A Long Way to Tipperary," a Basque rebel song. How appropriate!

No one asking for my real passport enables me to obtain my pilgrim passport immediately. Yet the town holds me for a few hours more of shopping. Socks, provisions and umbrella all obtained in a downpour, I pray (or hope) all the while for the heavy weather to lift. It does.

Before exiting Our Lady's Gate to enter on pilgrimage proper, I pause at La Chapelle de Notre Dame to light a candle for my mom, also Mary, as she'd like. Can't hurt.

5:15 p.m., 5 km Later

The Jacobean Way halts me here, after an hour of steady climbing, not to catch my breath but to tell you about the peculiarity of the Pyrenees. Now that I can claim bona fide pilgrim status, I can (and should) pause for your benefit. Whatever happens from here on, I am proud to have reached this point, to call myself "peregrino."

I've never seen the like of these Pyrenees, and yet I have. Picture the rolling green hills of Ireland, or Maryland, topped by great slabs of the scrubby brown mountains of Southern Cal. Surprisingly, American cornfields ride drumlin waves. Ripe and ready, the crop waits untouched in October. No sign of the harvest equipment or containers required.

Skirting the fields, bountiful and beautiful hardwoods stretch and climb up slopes. I pen this page beneath the arms of a monstrous ancient chestnut tree. Even employing my brelly and staff, I could not reach halfway around the trunk. Napoleon's men must have passed under these limbs and gathered marrons. I'll pick a souvenir for me. One of the stunted little nuts will do.

Charlemagne could have dropped the nut that sprouted here. His famously rash nephew, Roland, certainly passed this way once. We know he never returned. Pity, I can't sing "The Song of Roland," a pilgrim favorite of old. I deliver the best I can: "Kelly the Boy from Killan" (1798).

A purple flower, wild native to this region, should be picked and pressed for a wilder Dulcinea by this wild passerby. I'll wait though, until I'm sure that won't endanger the bloom or me.

- - - - -

Above the hills, below the peaks, the mountains of Erin fit neatly into the Pyrenees. Sheep trails and wee shitty roads (literally) wind unexpectedly through heather, bracken, bramble, nettle and gorse, of course. With all these Irish plants present, a cool damp climate must belong too. Or the Little People play tricks on me again.

No, I know I'm not in Erin, as folks bell their flocks here. The sweet silence of Irish glens this peregrino prefers. Moreover, soaring high over all (particularly that pilgrim) huge vultures wheel. Not very reassuring, they're definitely not Irish. Most remarkable in this broad landscape, the absence of other pilgrims almost alarms. Several, spotted in town below, probably populate the refuge above, but none has been seen en route, before or behind.

- - - - -

About a dozen sat to dinner when I arrived at my destination, Le Refuge d'Orrison, just before dark (7:30 p.m.). This hostel furnished hearty food, authentically Basque rabbit stew. Delicious camaraderie also satisfied all, until the "lord of the manor" (a temp) decided to hold court. Expounding in French to a captive audience, he annihilated all conversation. *Bonne nuit.*

11/10/07

As beans before bed (never *une bonne idée*) troubled my slumber, I rose early, hoping to salvage from my misfortune at least a dawn-lit departure. 7:30 to 8:00 a.m. holds fast on breakfast at the refuge though. Still, 8:30 found me walking, one of the first out. Not bad for the first day.

Hiker's Tip: Good news, anyone without my allergy difficulties (flour and fungi) need not pack a peck of food into these mountains. Wish I had known that. But beware the bones in bunnies.

10:30 a.m.

Passing two hours, I passed a middle-aged couple from Sligo, Ireland, who'd exited afore me. Though they strike me as toffs, I sang for them *The Irish Volunteer* ("the divil take the nobility"). They seemed to appreciate it, regardless, plus my favorite Irish joke. I knew they would at least understand the latter, being familiar with the Irish personalities inserted into an old "a priest, a minister, and a rabbi" joke. The Irish version delivers a one-two punch line.

I also swept by the fine Dutch fellow who rose early. He's no Flying Dutchman. Not surprisingly, mountains don't suit him. Having reached the top, I'm stopping now, at the first trail marker to list the distance to Santiago. A stone slab resembling a headstone informs me of 765 km to go. If my mind calculates correctly and my physique holds up, I can do that in time.

If I can't, if it kills me, the Pyrenees look so like Ireland, feel free to bury me here, by this stone near the fountain spring of the ill-fated Roland.

12:30 p.m.

In air far thinner than Ireland's, my muscles gladly start to descend from the clouds after so much climbing. No sooner had I caught my breath, my first view of Roncevaux Abbey took that breath away again.

The cloisters look more like a fortress, and surely someone used it as such, since *Roncevaux* is synonymous with *slaughter*.

Not only was Roland waylaid here in 778 (likely by Basques, not Moors), his historical monument has emblazoned on it "ETA" (Basque I.R.A.). Nearby nestles the neatest nastiest machine-gun nest ever met (empty for now).

I'm relieved to leave an area renowned for brutality to invaders (martial or religious). A hundred hunting blinds fortify the ridge above, solely for slaughtering harmless migrating birds. Shotguns popping always suggest "Duck!" to me, not duck hunting (or finch ambushing).

Really relieved to arrive at Roncevaux Abbey before my projected best time, I stop to eat. Lost time I will quickly regain by carrying less ungainly weight. Leaving my pack under St. Jim's protection, behind his rococo altar in the abbey chapel, allows exploration to follow freely.

- - - - -

Having lunched a lot and learned a load, in an inspiring setting, I return to suit up before the side altar. I feel like a matador or knight before battle. Oddly, my pack does feel lighter now, indicating either a miracle or thievery. At this point, I don't even care which.

- - - - -

Passing the Irish couple again, I let out more lyrics and laughs from Ireland. I try to leave them laughing, but the male half looks happy only to see me go. Not real peregrinos, they merely hill-walk here for a few days.

Hans, on the other hand, a young German, has hiked for four months. Sadly, I'm reminded (by the above border defenses) that before WWII, German youth hiked all over Europe in the name of "brotherhood." Hans doesn't worry me though.

- - - - -

Beware of Auritz. Without warning, the way veers right. The sole sign hides high up on a building (for the first time), blocked by scaffolding on another building. The footpath draws one's attention precisely when a pilgrim needs to look up. The entire sidewalk in the town remains exceptionally medieval. I had also turned the wrong way after the abbey, diverted by a path identically marked for pilgrims. An ancient spring supposedly commands our interest. Should not all side paths be clearly marked as such?

Again I gave the Irish couple a marching song, but the only joke jumps out from my getting lost twice (plus from still passing them twice).

- - - - -

Sure, siesta seems quaint, a genuine folk custom to cherish. Ain't it a bit long though? All shops closing exactly when most needed grows tiresome quickly.

Biskarret, 6:00 p.m.

What's really un-Irish in this landscape? The absence of bogs means no peat stains the streams here. "Crystalline" describes every brook. Something else unfortunately not Irish found here fortunately, the lack of litter (from locals or visitors) honors Spain and stains Ireland more.

Total care taken of the trail, and of those using it, impresses. You notice immediately if local standards slip. After taking a wrong turn, I recognized my mistake within 100 yards: (1) no signpost or yellow arrow appeared any-where; (2) the path underfoot turned substandard. A hiker would walk many miles in Ireland before concluding that a badly maintained trail meant he erred.

How else does one know this trail could not go through Ireland? Spain appears not to permit evergreen clear-cutting. Anyone wanting to work for the Irish tourist board (*Borde Failte*) should be required to visit clear-cut sites. If he or she doesn't cry, scream, or hit somebody, no job should follow. After that vetting, give them a backpack and orders to report back after they hike and hostel around both Ireland and Iberia.

The I.T.B., a government agency, should look out for ordinary folk on both sides of the tourism industry. Bigwigs can look out for themselves. Unfortunately, government ministers and bureaucrats prefer to hobnob with the mucky-mucks.

11/10/07; 8:15 p.m.

Boys and girls, what's done took some doin'. Arriving in St. Jean on the afternoon train yesterday, I found the walled town besieged by rain. After shopping for essentials, I set out too late at 4:00 p.m. My minimum destination attained, what should have served as my initial goal did not appear until this afternoon, leaving less than an afternoon to hotfoot to where I might have hit on day 1: Zubiri. Dammit, I did do it, though that meant running for miles, fully packed. The last hour took me on a dark path through a pine forest, on a mountain in a foreign country (sans passport) where I could not even see markers or understand spoken directions.

Crossing the stone bridge into the village, I did not know whether to collapse or dance. Securing a bed in an excellent hostel still required effort. On the free Internet provided, I looked up the song "The Impossible Dream," whose lyrics had played tag in my brain all day.

For today's success I credit excessive adrenaline and you, worthy reader. You push me on. I wouldn't want to disappoint. You'd feel let down if I allowed other hikers to pass me. No? OK, that's my own character flaw. That weakness makes me stronger though, when I need it.

In addition to every Irish rebel tune I know, the Spanish countryside will now ring, more appropriately, with the following. Too bad about the voice. I sing anyway, as Don Quixote the "Man of La Mancha," would.

"To dream the impossible dream,
to fight the unbeatable foe..."

This song becomes the theme of my camino unexpectedly, as I have always hated it for representing the faux ideals disguising the disgusting real-politicks of the Kennedy Camelot. Impossible dreams sent many young men to die in the morass of Vietnam. Yet in my old age, I rediscover idealism stolen from my youth. Idealism can grow dangerous, but mine will kill no one but me, another Man of LaMancha.

12/10/07; 8:00 a.m.

An even better song propels me from the hostel:

I am I, Don Quixote, the man of LaMancha.
My destiny calls, and I go...

I am amazed at my ability to maintain this pace. Everywhere I have gone for a fortnight, strangers sniffle and sneeze about me and then insist on shaking hands and sharing food. Not one proper night's rest has graced that time. Despite strange beds in noisy dorms, after long stress and hard traveling, I still stand, remarkably pain-free for fifty-three...Did I just jinx myself?

At least I managed to start the same time as yesterday, but no earlier.

Immediately outside Zubiri, the most satanic mill imaginable challenges all comers: "Beware! You are about to traverse Magna, S. A. Industrial site. Do not leave the path."

Oooh, fightin' talk. Lucky for Magna, destiny presses Don Q onward to Santiago.

I fear having failed already this morning the code of either knight errant or peregrino.

Of four Korean pilgrims who bunked with me last night, the youngest, Pearl (twenty-five), glows most smilingly and friendly. Attempting to compliment them all, I report, "Koreans are called the Irish of Asia." Aside from sharing a long history of conquest and partition, both nations came through with similar attitudes of good cheer and hospitality intact. These particular Koreans face personal oppression cheerfully. Sneezing and coughing all night, they offered breakfast to me in the morning. Yummee. Inclined to decline, not wishing to offend, I proffered my precious Swiss chocolate again. [The Way is hard.] Though the Koreans left well ahead of me, I found one, an older woman, waiting outside town. Waiting for me? Already running, I barreled by. She looked disappointed. Later I met her male companion coming back for her. Don't ask me.

- - - - -

I'll have you know I did turn back later for the Koreans. One hill already climbed I retrod to a tricky crossroads. I must have misheard their approach however, or an evil sorcerer trifles with me. Koreans never showed.

TIP! Lack of traditional hats and staffs among pilgrims shocks me. How foolish! **Second tip:** Bring a newspaper. (1) Sitting on cold hard rock can be brutal on your bum. (2) Disposable reading material. (3) When you have the runs and run short... (4) Best of all, raveled newspaper in hiking boots absorbs water, sweat and odor during the night!

12:30 p.m.

I'm also surprised to pass the other two Koreans, halfway to Pamplona. They march with that steady determination of Asian women. I pass pilgrims now who started in the next town. Two Canadian pilgrims, their scallop badges misplaced, sure do ensure their maple leaves show.

I slip by a German couple before Villava, a town surprisingly reminiscent of Ennistymon, Co. Clare. In a different, ugly way, Crossmaglen, Co. Armagh, comes to mind. Anyone ever in "Bandit Country"(for Brit soldiers) will know what I mean. The graffiti looks very similar.

I arrived just in time for a parade on the feast day of a local saint. This saint apparently appreciated dancing with massive papier-mâché figures, to rather raucous music.

Pamplona, capital of separatist Euskadi, approaches. Three Italian pelegrini seen here look like they have hiked from Rome. One looks like having left Glasgow, on a drunken dare, totally unprepared. No hat among them, broken tree limbs serve to support their own lame limbs. The "Scottish" bloke's face matches his flaming hair and beard. Haltingly, he follows his friends.

CHAPTER 2
Pamplona to Burgos, Spain

12/10/07; 2:15 p.m.

Pamplona surprises because of media induced preconceptions. No rustic village here, where locals follow the rural custom of running from bulls. Pamplona presents a pilgrim with a sprawling cosmopolitan metropolis. Capital and cathedral city for centuries, its Old Quarter remains the most impressively walled city I've ever set eyes on. The bulls, gone months ago, seem totally superfluous for making life interesting or exciting here.

A tasty inexpensive meal, enjoyed in a café, would have thrilled had it been what I ordered. Fine restaurants lining the Grand Plaza Del Castillo appear more dear. Off the square, the sign of El Bodega Hemingway undoubtedly read differently when himself wrote books there.

My left leg cramps painfully here in Pamplona. I'm relieved the bulls left in July.

5:30 p.m.

Met the Irish pair one final time in the tourist info office. They sought a train to a plane. I'm still walking, barely, with no notion why my left leg suddenly seizes up. Exiting the next town after Pamplona, I directly face a ridge lined with 100 threatening windmills.

I may fancy myself as Don Quixote, but never Custer.

8:30 p.m.

To reach the milling horizon took two hours of climbing into a setting sun. The cleverly designed trail brings pilgrims right across the mountain face, beneath the noses of the giants standing guard, as if puny people never meant to pass through such imposing ranks. Gradually, the way climbs to suddenly break through the sentry line before anyone can turn to stop intrepid or impudent intruders.

Never fleeing in the failing light, I initiated a flank attack. No refuge in sight, uphill I charged, swinging my hickory stick. Whack! The first big fella felt it badly. Stepping back, I dared him to challenge my passage. Noting his mates made no move to aid him, he pretended not to notice me. Well, a big swig of water I took then, as cool as you please, and turned my back on him. Limping away, I tried not to show less than fighting fitness. I would have battered him better, but for pity. On only one good leg myself, I felt bad for the big boyo who had only one leg ever to stand upon.

Another long path in the dark to the nearest hostel followed. Literally "out of the woods" this time, I hobbled into trouble. I fear we'll enjoy no more running on this trip. That's troubling because I've always managed to run from any trouble into which my feet misstep.

I swear I never did anything foolish in Pamplona. I didn't even pretend to run with bulls, or heifers even. Sitting too long for service in the little bistro may be to blame. The lighter weave of the slacks worn today might suffice to explain. Dehydration supplies the most likely culprit.

I will admit to larking through the mountains yesterday, dismissing the aches of others. Maybe God desires to remind me of the underlying bond of humanity: frailty. "OK, Lord, I get the point. Now, give me back my legs."

- - - - -

With pride truly curbed, a cripple would not have limped on from Pamplona to his designated destination. Permitting no peregrino or power-walker, day-hiker or dog-walker, to pass, vanity served more than insanity however. The spur supplied I have needed twice to avoid being stranded in the middle of nowhere in the night.

13/10/07; Sat. 11:30 a.m.

Well, I have tried to learn a lesson of some sort. This morning I departed late deliberately (near 11:00) after a long hot shower seemed to improve the leg. The Mexican, Jose, with whom I'd shared the dorm chose the opposite tack. Also badly hobbled, he had gone on even before I woke.

From two Californian girls passed near the hostel, I can hear gabbling behind me. They look lame too (only literally) and very fine of limb just the same.

- - - - -

Morning near gone, mist rising from the valley leaves those windmills, on hills behind me, standing on clouds. Fairly light of foot myself this morning, I make good progress. The leg stays gimpy, but I have developed the gait of a drunken sailor, allowing me to roll along without pain. This locomotion hampers forward motion though. *Adelante! Por Dios y Santiago!*

Don't believe any malicious, unfounded rumor about me tumbling off "the wagon," the one conveyance permitted to pilgrims. Wine would probably provide a better lift.

I've lost the California girls. They must have taken a wrong turn—like most Cal-gals.

- - - - -

Obanos, now left regrettably, gave me a great *tortilla de potatas* for brunch. All this eating of strange foods, on-the-go, with indecipherable ingredients, not to mention mystery water, should mean my insides would likely cripple me. I never expected my legs to quit first.

Anyway, this village looks very pleasantly laid out. The central church, once again, pilgrims find locked. Spain continues to disappoint on this point.

1:30 p.m.

An even more engaging village, on market day especially, Puente del Riena (Bridge of the Queen) provides necessary supplies: food, a replacement for the purse lost in Biarritz, a new pouch for valuables. My old pouch just fell apart inside my pack! I could easily have lost my essentials had I worn the pouch. Explain that without the devil or the Wee People.

3:30 p.m.

The Cal-gals reappeared behind me at the market and amazingly, did not stop to shop. They must feel right at home in the countryside just past that town. Parched hills, covered with vineyards, are crowned by mission villages. I felt drawn to Ciranqui, who (for an old lady) climbs with amazing grace up her hill. The church perched atop, though plain white stucco outside, displays golden rococo within.

The weather even in October feels like Southern Cal too. Much too hot for a Mick. Yes, I do confess to leaving my sunblock in rainy France.

Hiker's Tip: Whichever arm is most sunbathed, drape it elegantly with your towel. That allows the towel to dry while keeping your skin moist—quite a turnabout for a towel.

8:45 p.m.

The entire character of the terrain and its usage alters in the next valley. Still like California, but far from the vineyards, this ground faces tilling on a grand scale. Either the locals have plowed over the pilgrim path, or they're too busy to mark it well. Either way, I have still attained my minimum objective for the day, Estella, and on schedule (7:15), despite starting late and stopping as the intriguing route required. Registered in the hostel by 7:30, this quick Mick beat a young athletic looking fella from Barcelona for one of the final beds. He had one knee wrapped in an ace bandage though. I may need to buy one of those myself.

I took my first bad fall today. Tired at end of day, with my pack heavily listing, I felt my right foot grabbed on a rough downhill trail. My bad left leg couldn't catch me in time. Don't worry though. My head broke my fall. No real damage done.

- - - - -

I like Estella for her stunningly posed churches and genteel aging. The town crumbles charmingly. Preserving Old World atmosphere must be Spanish government policy. Otherwise, consumers could be better served. No Wal-Marts here. Pity people cannot seem to get what they need without mega-controllers, one way or the other. One oddity of consumption here (i.e., not odd here) dictates entering bars for snacks and ice cream. In these snack/booze bars, smoking remains de rigueur, unlike in Ireland or New York anymore. If that's not bad enough health-wise, restrooms never offer soap. You would swear a soap scare or scarcity sweeps across Spain.

Another thing, the country buzzes full of flies—in October—with not one screen seen. Every WC keeps the lights on one-minute timers. Do you see the problem here? Incidentally, the special peregrino menus offered everywhere do not generally come from a goodness of heart or a special devotion to St. Jim. If you dine, their dog may go hungry. Exceptions prove the rule.

Hiker's Tip: Have your own soap ready. Did you bring enough for the entire restaurant staff?

9:45 a.m. Sun. 14/10/07

I'm obliged to state I do not recommend the Albergue Municipal in Estella, not with other ones available. Big and basic would describe it. I'd add: less than welcoming. Sleep deprivation may sour my outlook though, as the German in the next bunk snored all night like a ripsaw when I needed to sleep like a log.

Excellently underway today, my leg feels miraculously better. I halt anyway, just outside town, to view the famous Irache Monastery, a must-stop for all pilgrims, as its fountain dispenses freely both water and wine! A large local producer provides the wine for peregrinos. Anyone not walking the way but still imbibing may choke on it and burn in hell.

Not all pilgrims also stop at the monastery's chapel. A Spanish couple I already passed bypass me now, but not before taking care to correct me: Basque, not Spanish.

This concern stands reflected everywhere. The entire countryside basks in Basque colors, flags and language, underscoring ETA graffiti. I'm amazed the territory isn't independent. What holds it? Not one Spanish soldier or policeman in sight, no Spanish flag flies, unless erected for desecration.

- - - - -

Sixteen persons I broke breaking for lunch: four Australian, three Canadian, one Frenchman, two Koreans, two Irish, two Danes, and the two Basques. I spoke to all and strode on. Surprisingly, none seem able to develop a gate designed to cover ground. This diary keeper, once a dairy keeper, stays a farmboy, one tempered by years in New York City. I can walk. I've got places to go, people to see, a plane to catch, and no time for lollygagging. Hardy's *The Mayor of Casterbridge* opens with a description of a countryman's walk. Partly due to injury, my gait evolves towards the low rocking style of the French Foreign Legion, famed for long desert marches.

Don't recall enlisting, but today feels like a forced march. I strained by no one after lunch because no one moves out here. One figure followed in the heat haze to the next town; no one ventured after that. One long slog over hard ground separates Los Arcos from Viana. No more the Irish marching songs, which entertained the girls in the cool of morning. Negro spirituals pull me through the afternoon. Nevertheless, I reached Viana before dark, precisely on target.

- - - - -

Hiker's Tip: I've learned that churches generally open only in summer, because a government stipend ensures a caretaker. Summer over, stipends finish, and churches close. Kinda sad.

Mon., 15/10/07

Injury #2: A big bruise appears mysteriously on my left shinbone. Looks like Lucifer himself hauled off and kicked me for defeating my initial injury. I'm probably more subject to bruising in my weak state. What really unsettles, the soreness does not settle but shifts downward as I move.

When I debooted in the albergue last night, a lump showed on the side of my leg where the boot rubs. On waking, I found injuries #1 and #2 improved, but #3 worse. If shin splints, it's worse than ever experienced in years of distance running. If the boots caused the problem, what can I do? They never gave trouble before. As every ounce of fat has fled my frame, the boots do not fit as they did. I tried lacing them differently. None of the hurt happened before that, or before I changed to lighter slacks and socks.

My difficulty springs from an inability to do the laundry. *Albergues* (refuges) claim to serve pilgrims, like the hospitals of old, but I find them quite unhelpful. If I spoke Spanish, I'd be better off, but that said, these providers must already know well the basic needs of hikers. They seem intent on not providing them, even when advertised. If offering laundry facilities, for instance, a hostel's sole machine probably sits broken, or its complicated operation or regulation goes unexplained. If a dryer even exists, it takes forever, plus a pile of change. Patience doesn't help, as unknown prior-claims or rules may take your turn. Never mind laundry soap, would providing a little hand soap kill a hostel? Its absence certainly might kill me. The lack of left-luggages endangers doubly. Only yesterday I heard pilgrims can get a special rate for mailing bundles to Santiago. I don't know if that's true. Probably ought not to post dirty clothes anyway.

One worries most about lock-out at 10 p.m.! I left late last night, due to doing laundry. Clean clothes can claim priority over food. Naturally, the machine broke as my turn came. After a fruitless struggle, I limped out to the nearest eatery. As service took longer than expected (though they did try), I hopped back faster, but not quick enough. Locked out, I lucked out as another guest let me in against the rules.

15/10/07; 1:20 p.m.

Setting out on a bad leg, under a load of dirty clothes, I expected to declare only I was passed on this tightly hobbled march. Actually, no one swept me; I dusted three (Swiss, Spanish) before the next town, Logano, where a laundromat required finding. Washing done, I looked for lockers in a bus station.

Petty as my game of passing people may seem, it becomes a useful gad for this heavily handicapped horse. After bounding over the mountains of Ireland for weeks (years even) without sign of weakness, I felt struck by misfortune as soon as I set foot in France. No Franco-phobe, I love La Belle France and expected no *malchance*. While having no desire to permanently cripple myself, I know no other way than to press on. I've heard of R.I.C.E.: rest, ice, compression and elevation. What about soaking in hot Epsom salts? I don't know. I have no ace bandage, and have heard that they restrict circulation dangerously anyhow.

10:00 p.m.

Ice chills it now. Swelling must be brought down. Not one step did I take today without pain. Viana to Logano, Logano to Navarette (plus one circuit of Logano), equals thirteen hours of hurt. I began feeling feverish from withstanding pain, alternating stab/throb. Fear of an untreated bite of an unknown bug bit into my brain. I imagined for miles asking for ice at the door of the albergue—if only I could reach the door. Following irregular markings in the dark on an unknown trail for hours will suffice for excitement tonight. No peregrino passed or was passed, as none felt fool enough to set off at that hour.

Staggering into Navarrete, I scan every building for a mile before finding the seashell sign. At a blessed lighted door, salvation finally comes. The warden speaks French, not Spanish. Better still, Jose, my Mex-Oz pal (and fellow cripple) greets me at the door. He's fluent in three languages (plus Aussie). Thirdly, the warden declares himself a dues-paying member of the Walking Wounded Club. He didn't understand much of my French but comprehends my pain *immediatément*. Seeing my lower leg swollen like a balloon rouses his empathy, personal and practical. Ice and first aid cream offered first, I accept the former and decline the latter. Sitting down with great relief, I find most comfort in confirmation of what went wrong and why.

Three days ago, noting that heavy weight loss left my boots loose, I (fearing blisters) had devised a different lacing method. What felt good and snug would prove bad and tight however. My boot top damaged tiny connective tissue on my shin, which inflamed and swelled. My new *bon ami* assures me hospital care, four days of R.I.C.E. (minimum), plus proper lacing will help.

My Mexican amigo could not believe I walked from Viana in that condition. He concludes all Irish people must be madly stubborn. He never knew how much of Logano I'd tramped too. My pack weighs way too much as well, as the station lockers cost too much cash and convenience.

Tues. 16/10/07 a.m.

This moment may mark the end of my Camino de Santiago. Offered free medical care and accommodation last night if I would remain in Navarrete, I must accept, or *mon ami le plus bon* will wash his hands of me and give up hope of my ever hiking to Santiago. Failing to appreciate that even a few days off the trail, followed by more of light travel, totals more than I can afford, he only knows my little injury is actually very serious. More inflammation means more swelling, causing less circulation and more damage, leading to more inflammation and more swelling.

At the clinic today the doctor wanted to inject my leg (cortisone?) and offered tablets as an alternative. I remain uncertain, however, that she understands the nature of my problem. Doctors don't listen even when you speak their language. As a free medical service, the level of care scarcely reaches exhaustive or enthusiastic. So, I'll just carry on with the rest-and-ice advice, which she confirms. She gave me aspirin too, to take before flying, due to the lethal threat of thrombosis, a danger I'd not even considered. Guess I can't walk, can't stay, and can't fly away.

I would like to note, though, that in Logano yesterday I received, due to my pilgrim status, gratis laundry detergent and pastries from two strangers. The latter treat of course poisons me. Yet, as she who offered would not know that, I ate it anyway—and may "pay" for it later.

You find me in the parish church of Navarrete, before the most ornate altarpiece I've ever seen—and I have seen plenty. Seventy kilos of Peruvian gold covers the entire sanctuary, wall-to-wall, floor-to-roof. Elaborate and intricate gold-plated carving merely frames sacred art. Holy Smoke! Was Pissaro himself a Navarrete boy?

I only came in because the hostel closes during the day, and nowhere else opens for free, especially during siesta. I must leave shortly, as my leg begins to throb, though I stay off it as much as possible. As the hostel will open soon, I will have somewhere to go on this unexpectedly chilly day. I'll try that ointment offered last night, after all. I could try praying for healing before leaving church, but you know my problem there. This much I can do:

On my sacred oath, whatever happens, whatever I can do today or tomorrow, win or lose, I shall return someday to this golden altar, to complete this pilgrimage, and repeat it doubly, if my legs heal. All along the route I will offer succor to others—fiscal, physical, psychological. All this I will do if God is here to help me. I swear it on my honor and on His holy altar.

7:00 p.m.

If that's not enough, it's the best I can do…aside from buying chocolates for all who hostel with me tonight. Returning to matters more mundane, though unable to walk anywhere, I still have the runs. Lucky I'm not going anywhere as I'm going everywhere. Beware dehydration.

Wed. 17/10/07

I have more reason to look more sourly on the entire universe this morning. A sound regimen planned for marching by tomorrow, I prepared to face the warden's insistence that I obey his instruction about resting my legs at least for four days, double what I could give. Instead, a totally different confrontation awaited. As the doors closed this a.m., the warden told me to go for good, then and there: *"Partir immediátément par la regulation."*

Apparently, I needed to obtain yesterday a note from the doctor in order to stay longer than two nights at any official albergue. As the M.D. had willingly offered injections and tablets, a bit of script should not have been problematic. However, when I presented my peregrino pass, as the warden had instructed, the clinic receptionist only looked at me like I was simple. More papers (permits or cash) she demanded before permitting any doctor to see me. When my Irish social services card finally did the trick, it produced no paper for me. Having allowed two minutes with an M.D., the dragon then ordered me to leave. You know the type all medicos like to keep chained in reception. Try one when you can't speak her language. Sca-r-y!

However, had the warden explained the need for a doctor's note, I'd have stayed to fight the dragon or returned to her den. Since the warden recognized my injury's serious-ness, he knew my need to avoid sudden stress, movement or lifting. If he had given any notice, or noticed bad behavior by me, I wouldn't mind. Due to his advice, I'd devised careful exercise to enable early departure—for naught. According to unposted rules, I'm not even able to leave my pack for a few hours in a locked hostel while seeking accommodation. "*C'est impossible,*" he repeats. Impossible? It's easy. Who would know? In English and French I told him he did evil.

Thank God the rain held off. None of this affects my vow though. *Au contraire*, I feel added need to protect pere-grinos from the organization meant to protect them.

- - - - -

What amazes most: my traipsing about Erin for years without a tenth of the trial this trail affords in a week. Every day, another problem surfaces. Makes me wonder.

Not a good night's rest has Morpheus granted in three weeks. Walking at all astonishes. No one to blame really. A new rule for shelters came to me in a dream though: snorers can be carried in their sleeping bags into the yard. I wouldn't care to fall victim to the rule myself and have heard that my snoring helped to put me on the road in the first place...

18/10/07

In Navarrete's other hostel, in the middle of the night, in the lighted loo:

Well, my darlin' dears, I fear these words will run towards dark night of the soul shit. Sorry to share. I'll keep it short. As you can see, I cannot sleep. Not sleeping well already, I just noticed a loss of circulation in my left foot. Maybe I eat too much chocolate, to make my mock meals more palatable. Contrary to everything I believe, I have been desperately seeking doctors, though they understand me even less than usual. Besides slapping on ice and over-the-counter anti-inflammatory creams, I pop aspirin—not for pain, to thin blood. All warnings, ingredients and directions appear as gobbledygook to me. Maybe both a bug bite and boot bite cause the problem, the latter due to the former (swelling causing rubbing, causing swelling). I probably should have accepted the hypo when offered. There's no going down that path now.

Worst of all, I face the sudden realization that, if I am lame and alone up a mountain (without even God to help me), I did really choose this path for myself, though I didn't know it. I don't think that excuses the "ex" entirely though.

Sometime today, ready or not, I am going to hit the road. Even the limping Italian Scot and Cal-gals have caught up, after my second day here. I'm taking that as a sign: time to go, even though one of those girls looks the very image of Angelina Jolie (only more *jolie*).

Regrettably, I am seldom mistaken for Brad Pitt. Did I tell you I met him once in Belfast? He researched for a movie about the I.R.A. I'll have to share that story with Angie-oh-so-jolie if we meet again. No, I'm not telling you. I'm saving that one for her—not that it'll do me any good.

11:30 a.m.

I have thrown away my map of Navarrete. I'm on my way. Naturally, the nearest refuge has closed. Ha! I'm for the next one now, or I'm just for it. Oh, and it looks like rain again.

I should have stopped at my hostel once more before leaving town, to beg for ice and salve. However, the landlady looked glad to see me go. As she spoke no English, my necessary queries only confused her. She never volunteered the fact that breakfast cost €3 extra either—until after I ate. At least she never chased me out before 8:00 a.m.

One thing I did do for my leg before leaving town: mailed to Santiago three kilos from my pack. At €6, that's the best bargain in Spain, believe me. I could have posted 5 kilos, but could not wring it from my pack and pouches. Anyone fool enough to carry more than 5 kilos extra over the mountains deserves to pay more, or pain more.

Hiker's Tip: Don't pay €2.50 for an official mailing box. Ask any shop for a good box.

Noon 18/10/07

Nearly an hour out from Navarrete, I'm still upright. The new stride, no longer the roll of a drunken sailor or the rock of a legionnaire, I call the Hitler Hop, since it lurches to the right. I swear by St. James I do not drunkenly reel through the wine country of Spain. If my right leg fails me too, I may yet turn to drink though.

I stop to take an aspirin. In my dehydrated damaged state, thinning the blood must improve circulation and healing. I stopped twice today already to mark the path more clearly for any who follow, something I have not done before. Stopping comes easier when you're moving slower.

2:20 p.m.

Whoa back! How's this for a howdy-do? Lurching along, minding my footfalls, I chance to notice my hands have turned a greenish tinge. I don't know if it's a product (physical or psychedelic) of salve employed or bug bites. Might be just a trick of the light in this odd countryside. I really don't much care. I feel better than I have in days, and I cover ground. If I'm dead, I don't give a damn.

Odder still: when I stopped to pen this note, I went to sit on a rock. From behind the boulder, in the middle of nowhere, a big black beast emerged to growl an invitation to hell. Deciding this devil dog might not be a figment of my feverish imagination, I elected not to sit down.

3:00 p.m.

Coming into Najera now. More on the previous incident: for the first time in years I had just sung "The Wearing of the Green" before I noticed my turning green. Weirder yet, when I failed to sit, due to the dog, I stood nearby to write. Moving off, I noted the back of my ankle hurt, as if bitten. What kind of dog can do that? I'm certain sure none of this is "just in my head." I've attained the town regardless without a soul slipping by, despite my stopping to fill up and let out. No sign of anyone on the road ahead. If wise, I'll stop at Najera hostel to smear on salve at least.

5:30 p.m.

Providence has kindly placed the next albergue 23 km away. That keeps me from overdoing and keeps me here in fascinating Najera. Odd caves locals carved into the cliffs above the town in the 10th century. A monastery of unmatched significance royalty established here too, as their burial place. Better still, a Spar Supermarket remains open today.

Hours after my arrival, Hans, the German schlepping tent and pack shows up, with a pleasant English woman now in tow. Happy to direct them to the municipal refuge and the Spar, I receive in return a tale from the lady.

Walking alone, this woman had become very fearful of many ferocious guard dogs and strays along the way, despite sharing the English passion for dogs. English canines carry no rabies though and generally act as restrained as their masters. Her fear began to morph into a phobia capable of halting her pilgrimage. Then, on a long stretch of lonely trail, she froze on hearing an unseen beast barking at her. Without even a stick to defend herself, she glanced about desperately. Finding no help, she saw no whelp either. Hoping she'd not gone barking mad, the lady hurried on. However, the barking struck a plaintive note that made her pause...

Trying again to locate the critter, and noting no dwelling near, her eye fell upon some agricultural plumbing beside the trail. Into this a terrier had leapt. Sheer walls of concrete pipe made exit impossible. Bloody forepaws and missing nails testified to the pup's best efforts.

Judging by the animal's sorry state, the human reckoned the pooch had passed at least one dry day in this man-made hole, where drowning presented the most likely threat. Fearing rabies or the reaction of any trapped animal (and wary of fleas and ticks), the woman knelt to help a fellow creature. The suffering recipient, instinctively aware of altruistic assistance, came gently and gratefully from the death-trap. From there, the woman walked away unafraid.

19/10/06; 8:00 a.m.

For me, the engrained fear would probably be of robbery in the rough hostels. Not all walkers are pilgrims; not all pilgrims are devout. Though some esprit de corps exists, I'd not depend upon it. I take precautions accordingly. The slacks used for PJs have pockets for stowing valuables. Maybe valuables on my mind, besides on my hip, keeps me awake. Mostly uneasiness can be traced to my troubled digestion.

Rising in the dark, at an unknown hour, to answer the call, I stumbled sleepily to the loo. Robbed of sleep, I nearly had sleep rob me. For, when I returned to my bunk, after wake-up bells and lights on, I found my wallet had fallen from my pocket to lie open on my bed...untouched.

Hiker's Tip: Bring a watch with a very bright light. I like little lighted magnifying glasses too.

19/10/07; 10:00 a.m.

Six pilgrims fell to my pace before the next village, though my right Achilles still hurts. One Spaniard, two Frenchmen, two Aussie, and the Celtic Iti, Dominico. I marched into town with him and a martial hymn. He manages much better now. My rebel tunes help him. Hope we meet again in Santiago. If we meet before that, I'm buying him a hat. He's burning up! No one should go abroad nowadays without a broad-brimmed hat.

12:30 p.m.

The next town is named for Dominic's namesake, St. Domingo, a great boon of pilgrims, from medieval times to today. This Camino town interests me most to date. In its cathedral a magnificent tomb of the saint competes with a chicken coop! Live hen and rooster! Employed in celebrating the saint's feast day, the birds don't figure in the feast. The town also treasures the oldest hostel on this ancient route. I mean to stay there next time.

Five more pilgrims my gimpy gait grabbed approaching Santo Domingo. Recall two Koreans with an Austrian? I'd like to meet again the Portuguese couple too, as the male speaks fluent English with an Irish accent, after a year in Dublin, a city favored by English language students.

Most pilgrims do speak English, but few wardens do. That's fine, but guidelines and guides should be posted in English (plus French and German) at every albergue.

- - - - -

After lunch I lumbered by another four peregrinos. The Dutchman out-stridden on Day One in the mountains remembers me. A total of three days off the trail by me had let him pass me. The most truly interesting pilgrim, one never passed, never passed me either…

Before Santo Domingo, the road climbs up long inclines on heavily cultivated hills. At the foot of one such slope, I stood scribbling when a wanderer suddenly appeared at my elbow. "Hola," I replied over my shoulder as I took off. From the corner of my eye, I perceived his shadow keeping pace, as did the crunch of gravel behind me. My glimpse of him had recognized the ethereal quality of a Buddhist or New Age cultist, capable of transcendental trance for moving effortlessly. "I'll show ya walkin'!" Thinks I, leaning into the grade with my staff. "You'll bring a stick next time." Without warning, hard wood started striking ground behind me.

Up the hill we powered together, never slacking. Not paining, he gained. Yet, I crested first to capture some dignity from defeat. At the brink of the hill and the rim of a town, I turned to discover a totally different person behind me. A bearded macho man stared back. Where did he come from? Do they lurk behind bushes to try me in relays?

Maybe God sends angels to test me. By beating the angels I fail the test. During the climb I expected punishment for my pride. Something in my frail frame felt bound to snap...

Au contraire, the shot of adrenaline and double oxygen loosened my limbs. By the top of the hill I had shifted into top gear, on top of pain. In the zone, I passed unpassed through town, and on to the next one. Though the mystery man tailed me, I even had time to eat lunch before his appearance pushed me out of that town. Glancing back again, I discovered he'd disappeared.

Striding well enough to skip albergues, I tramped on under a blistering sun until my feet blistered, my sights set on El Cid's fortress town, Belorado.

Taking care to stop before stamina broke, or legs buckled, I noted my left leg began to swell before I braked at the first hostel though it offered no first aid kit. Ice must suffice.

20/10/07 Belorado

Why did I bet myself that I could rest in Burgos today? After injury, I should take more care, but due to the injuries, I can't afford care. Gotta fly soon, or crash and burn. Burgos commands one of the magic names on El Camino. Not only does the burg possess great historic importance on the route, in the psyche of peregrinos Burgos marks the halfway point, but not in reality. For tourists the city affords a bright high-point. I just feel, after days of inaction, if I fail to wake up there tomorrow, passing it tomorrow (or ever) grows unlikely. Besides, the hostel hostess and my two pro-trekker roommates said I couldn't do it.

First, let me seek the assistance of El Cid. The biggest albergue in town nestles in the final remnant of his castle. Stopping here for anti-inflammatory cream, I view a shelter as quaint and historic as the rest of this captivating town. Next time, I stay here, though they have no salve.

Hoping last night's ice does suffice, I pause already to breakfast in a café on the central square. The two French super-hikers catch me here. Though I got the jump on them this morning, they'll have a head start now, because my dietary needs require more care in ordering.

- - - - -

Striving to catch the Frenchmen, I overtake the two girls from Oz, dusted days ago when healthier. Can't say I'm disappointed at finding them instead. This brace of sheilas win my award for favorite pilgrims. Aside from pretty and witty, they are—like all Aussies—natural born pilgrims. God bless 'em all.

Their charming conversation comforted me. They assure me that I am not alone in travail. They, and everyone they've met, have experienced exceptional physical difficulties and freaky obstacles. I rewarded them with another song, "The Spalpeen's Lament," detailing trials worse than ours and explaining why so many Irish sailed to America and Australia.

One evening of late as I happened to stray,
to the county Tipperary I did make my way,
To dig the potatoes and work by the day
for a farmer called Darby O'Leary.
I asked him how far we were bound for to go,
the night being dark, and a cold wind did blow.
I was tired and hungry; my spirits were low,
for he'd give neither whiskey nor water.

This dirty old miser, he mounted his steed.
To the Galbally Mountains he rode with great speed.
I followed behind till my poor feet did bleed,
and we stopped when his old horse grew weary.
When we came to his cottage, I entered it first,
though it looked like a kennel or a ruined old church.
Says I to myself, I am left in the lurch,
in this house of old Darby O'Leary.

I well recollect it was Michaelmas night,
to a fine hearty supper, he did me invite:
One cup of sour milk that was more green than white,
and it gave me the trotting disorder.
His wet old potatoes would poison the rats, the barn, where
my bed was, was swarming with bats.
The fleas would have frightened the fearless St. Pat,
who banished the snakes o'er the border.

He worked me by day, and he worked me by night,
while a bit of old candle he held for some light.
I wished his potatoes would die of the blight,
or himself would go off with the fairies.
Upon this old miser I looked with a frown,
when wet straw he brought in for to make my shake-down.
I wished that I'd never seen him nor his town,
nor the sky over Darby O'Leary!

Shortly afterwards, I ran into the Irish couple introduced in Estella. I'd let them pass in Navarrete. Joining in on the litany of injury, they agreed that the primary problem is dehydration. The weather does not feel oppressively hot usually, but dry air sucks moisture from our bodies. Sweat evaporates before you notice it. The difference in oxygen levels and air pressure, due to the altitude change from Ireland, also affects us. Even the plains of Castile rest on a high plateau.

- - - - -

When passing the young, gracious French couple cycling El Camino, I assumed they would sweep me shortly. However, the route from Villafranca turns hilly and rough, like Irish terrain again. Specifically, hillsides of scrub oak, topped by evergreen plantations, recall Glendalough. Heather and gorse reappear. The difference? Again, no sign of ugly clear-cutting! The conifers look native and nicely spaced.

At one point a large hound lurking by the path made me nervous, until I discerned his occupation (and his boss nearby): truffle hunter. Imagine spying that near any larch crop in Ireland.

- - - - -

Though *les cyclistes* did eventually overtake me, I outdid them again, plus that Danish pair, the best hikers met so far. At least a dozen others my legs left in those woods: Brazilians, Canadians, Spaniards. None of these have met me before, I'm very happy to say.

- - - - -

San Juan de Ortega stopped me dead. Nothing in this remote hill village prepares the passerby for its remarkable chapel. My favorite to date, this church/mausoleum you'll need to see for yourself. I've already said too much, spoiling the surprise. The trail to it surprises too, bestowing the most shade so far.

- - - - -

I'm proud to outstrip a young Swiss couple. Good walkers, they probably carry too much weight (as careful Swiss tend to do). A German, a Frenchman and a Finn were easier, even before a high hill combined Gethsemane with Golgotha. Sure enough, a large concrete cross graced the top. A long downhill follows, making me nearly run, a first for days. As I flew past the old Koreans, they promised me a precious Pearl upon the path ahead.

Failing to surface with a pearl from my downhill dive, I did find the Austrian chess player, a treasure of great measure. He's stopping at the albergue there and warns I can't make Burgos. If I hadn't posted my chess set to Santiago, I probably would have stayed, more fool I. He thinks me foolish for pushing on at this hour, but it's Burgos or bust for me now—more likely the latter.

- - - - -

Yellow arrows can drive you mad too. Construction just caused me to make a large loop. Driving, you don't mind a couple extra kilometers. Wasted walking hurts.

I've landed in a suburb of Burgos now. Though darkness has descended, streetlights and sidewalk will guide me all the way in. An albergue shouldn't be too hard to find. I'd be there now had I not stumbled on a restaurant with the best tortilla to date. The toilet represents a rarer find, accessible even when handicapped with a pack. Soap too! I would love to eat breakfast at this "Tiffany's" but must move on. Tiffany's allowed that Finn to slip by me. I suspect a shortcut helped him too. That's OK. With the limp on him now, I'll not see his back again.

All right already, as soon as I locate a hostel, I'll go back to bring him in.

- - - - -

Nope, I never did go back—because I barely beat curfew myself. The grace of God alone, and an interesting alleyway, led me to a refuge near Cathedral Square. See, curiosity isn't always fatal. The real municipal hostel, once again, sits on the far side of the city. Why do they do that?

Never mind, I said Burgos, and Burgos this is—and over 50 km that was. Oh, the two French fellows chased all day? Unwittingly left at the first cantina!

That's all the good news; the bad news is my catching up with the famous snore factory. I can't even gripe, as my late preparations for bed, and this scribbling, keep everybody else awake.

21/10/07 Sun.

Only a few days ago, I began a letter home with this joke: "You find me seated with my feet up, at the open window of a café in sunny Spain."

That's funny as I sat in the café only because I was unable to walk. My feet I elevated to reduce swelling in the legs and to apply makeshift icepacks. The window opened on an unexpectedly cold day because smoking remains required in Spanish cafés. Rather than happily relaxing, I wallowed in worry and misery, since walking to Santiago, or anywhere, might never happen. One bug bite, or tight boot, could consign me to the bus, like many others before. This pilgrimage produces a parade of suffering and sorrow.

Now, I sit in another café, on a fairy-tale square, before a great cathedral. I'm 100 km away from the above misery, and I walked here, 55 km, in a day. Sure my leg still hurts, and I have other concerns, but I tread over them grimly. Yesterday, a sudden stop on loose gravel saved me from a hit and run when blinded by the sun, but blinding pain made me want to step in front of a car. My true desire, one good night's sleep, I denied myself by marching to meet a legendary snorer. Something I ate has caught up with me. Should I stride another 50 km today to evade the chainsaw massacre tonight? No. Today Burgos blushes before me, and I'll enjoy her charms before deserting her but will also attend high Mass in the cathedral, like a good pilgrim of old.

This cathedral holds the last, final resting place of El Cid. Mr. and Mrs. Cid lie beneath a simple slab, but the entire edifice forms the most drop-dead gorgeous mausoleum ever visited. An ornate lacework dome above the tomb, Emperor Philip II neatly described as "More the work of angels than of men." Yet I've never heard Burgos listed among the great cathedral cities or rated as a city of culture. For boulevarding amidst art, fashion and history, try Burgos.

Judging by the throngs in the streets at 10:00 p.m. and the street noise heard until 6:30 a.m., Burgos could claim party-town status too, on Saturday night at least. I know a certain senorita who would love to party here, in a new pair of kick-ass Spanish boots.

CHAPTER 3
Burgos to Leon, Spain

3:00 p.m., Sun.

Though an hour behind schedule for departing, I wouldn't care except... Feeling relaxed and rested, I knelt, without thinking, to look in my pack. An audible cracking noise finished in a louder yelp from me. As God loves irony, I had bent down to find aspirin.

Still able to hobble, I needed to run to the loo. Before finishing, with a flourish and a flush, I realized that the gum I chomped included a chunk of molar. Seemingly, wrecking my legs to run up doctor bills will not suffice for suffering. My dental health now depends on me halting my camino. Dentists too want to drill into my wallet. Well, I ain't stoppin'.

- - - - -

I reckoned that enough bad luck for one day. Three strikes and you're out. No, after that I met a man from Miami who knew the Yankees had lost the pennant—to the Red Sox. Worse, the Sox had come from behind to play game 7 in the World Series. Yikes! This'll render all Sox fans insufferable. Maybe it's good luck I'm in another world and nearly the next world.

Hobbling out of Burgos, I noted that public authorities, and the public in general, seem determined to create surprising little steps in the pavement—just enough to catch the toe or heel of a hiking boot. Jesus, Mary and Joseph!

How it does hurt! Stopping at the municipal hostel for help, I located none. None not too involved for me to use. Onward I inched, hoping to suffer alone at that late hour. Nope, four ladies had to trail me to the next town. By then I felt warmed up enough to struggle to the next, as the first refuge promised no anti-inflammatories.

Naturally the next shelter sat farther away than good sense would attempt, but if I could reach it, as originally planned, my late start and lame leg would have been totally surmounted. Hornillos del Camino became my target, as the actual next albergue had closed, of course.

Funny, having spent the whole day hiding from the Spanish sun, suddenly I chased it, hoping to view it again at the top of each rise, or, even better, the twinkling lights of a village. Finally, the last line of light died on the horizon with my last hope.

Trail markers wane invisible in the twilight. Then must a wayfarer plead with luck, if he cannot pray, to let him see any light or sign of hope. After the next rise, a great plateau stretches into total darkness. Only empty night surrounds...

Your feet tell you first. When night falls that black, your feet inform you when you start downhill. Then a fluvial depression might suddenly open in that high plain. There a delightful light might wink at the wanderer. A wee village waits, Hornillos del Camino, and maybe God.

Hontanas, 22/10/07, Mon.

Two hawks stooping I watch today, and more quail than I can shake a pilgrim's stick at. This region looks so rustic, so

Old World, you feel yourself break a time barrier merely walking through here. History or "progress" has depopulated rural Spain worse than Ireland. Entire villages scarcely amount to more than piles of abandoned adobe rubble. Some signs of a recent influx of capital glimmer here and there. Is El Camino the conduit? Hontanas appears, another secret in a hidden valley. I may aim for the albergue here next time—but never at night!

11:30 a.m.

Where busy road passes under arches of San Anton, that ruined nunnery impresses still, oppresses even. Only the hilltop castle beyond imposes more. El Cid, one might imagine sallying forth from that fortress.

Even scarier, but not imposing, the little old lady hiking behind me impresses. All hikers in last night's hostel your crippled correspondent had long since hobbled by when a backward glance recognized a tall German girl mounting a comeback. Eating breakfast on the move, I resented and resisted her relentlessness. Meeting monsters that Don Quixote never faced (combine harvesters and road-graders), I battled through to the next village ahead of pursuit, and presumed time to purchase ice cream and water.

In no time, gliding behind me into the cantina, a petite older Eurasian woman landed gracefully, birdlike, not the tall Teutonic girl expected. Here's a real trekker; I only pretend. She chased me all the way to the next town, but dropped the tail to siesta in Castrojeritz (Castroharris).

2:00 p.m.

Even the giants with flailing arms stood back astutely during my epic 55 km trek, two days ago. They pretended to

54

taunt me, but from a safe distance. Today, an entire troop of them stand stock still, holding their breath, hoping I don't notice them as I stride by—without a limp, despite my damaged leg and blistered feet.

I cover ground pretty well now. On the steep bluff beyond Castrojeritz, I could spot only one cyclist in the vista behind me. Betting myself that, on a grade, I could beat the cyclist to the crest, I leaned into the slope, and into the hope that adrenaline might boost my legs and lungs.

Not only did I crest first, I crossed the mesa, clambered down the far side, and traversed a broad plain, as far as the eye could see. Only when I had stopped at a peregrino rest area, to note my triumph, did the cyclist roll up. I shared my chocolate with him. He's Italian, but not one of their famous pro-cyclists. A taxi-driver, used to Irish tourists, he gave me the "slainte" salute.

Still no sign of any other life on the trail, or off it—except for flies. I gotta fly.

7:00 p.m.

Funny, ain't it, how coming in October worried me so? Now, I'd not try any other time. There's a life lesson. I just crossed an empty desert, albeit fully cultivated. Today's tramp across the high plains of Castile matched what I'd imagined the entire camino to be—except for the intensity and scale of agriculture. Every acre of arable land rolls under the plow. Either agri-business or government must direct this. Spain apparently provides the breadbasket of Europe. **Hiker's Tip**: reread previous paragraph.

- - - - -

I did get to view one old shepherd with a wandering flock, and a donkey standing guard over one lost lamb. I couldn't guess how the jackass would respond to my approach, but he may have wondered the same thing. Well into the next province now, Leon, I should hit a big town tomorrow when shops start opening. A village, Boadilla del Camino, presents a good place to stop today, with a choice of albergues.

I admit being tired, and a bit disheartened, as I just witnessed the woman whose walking I had admired being dropped off from a tractor at the hostel before me. Maybe she'll return tomorrow to where she quit today? Hmpff...maybe.

I've witnessed worse. On my first night on the camino, the writer of a guidebook told me that many new guides appear yearly with pages copied directly from other guides, or merely translated. A few days later, I watched an American copy pages from a guidebook into his "journal." When I ribbed him, he left in a huff. Maybe he does seriously plagiarize. He admits to not walking the whole Camino. Such is the world, but El Camino remains untouched.

More depressing, despite my half day off with my bad leg, I have again caught up with Senor Snorer. My goal for tomorrow becomes to reach any albergue after one where he stops. Sleeping in such close proximity with strangers, or not sleeping, must catch up with me soon.

23/10/07, Tues. 8:00 a.m.

Roosters crowing, cows lowing, church bells tolling, all in town (Boadilla). Walking in predawn dark, I'm hoping not to miss any of the yellow arrows pointing the way.

Fumista:

Six km before breakfast. Stopped for groceries and anti-inflammation cream. Pilgrims passing. Gotta run. Oh, that's right, I can't run.

- - - - -

Shortly after Fumista, the clouds let go and gave me the opportunity to steal a march. No, not on a tractor. Having come armed with an umbrella and a pack-cover, I could keep walking, quite dry, for hours. Others were unprepared or over-prepared. Ever try hiking when fully kitted in rain gear? You're soon wringing wet inside and out. All peregrinos should practice in Ireland for rainy day trekking.

Just two towns up the line, my goal line appears. The Wagnerian snorer calls halt here. Carrion, the next large town, calls me to carry on.

- - - - -

Yes, I did... I did carry on past Carrion, as did the rain too. Too damn much daylight dallied to let me rest. Is there too damned little daylight to reach the next town? Calzadilla stands infamously far off. I might be better off not doing so well.

Outside Carrion a sign posts a do-able distance to Calzadilla. Only afterwards did I decide that sign designated highway miles. Happy in my ignorance, and still nearly dry, I set off. However, after nearly twelve hours of walking in the rain, two hours in the dark on a muddy track, alone in an unknown land, I no longer felt dry, or happy.

No, cheeky devil, I'm not happy in the Irish weather. In sweet Erin rain never pours like this. Besides, as I crossed a flat plain of well-plowed fields, separated by lines of poplars,

Poland came to mind, before deep darkness covered all. I have never been out in a night like it.

With no hope of moonlight, some memory of light remained in the clouds to make the wet path glimmer, but no glow graced any horizon. No light of God or man showed, though the view opened unobstructed for 360 degrees. Each intersecting path toyed with my mind, but each time every arrow, if found in the darkness, repeated "Forward…"

After almost 20 km without sign of human habitation, the plain unexpectedly drops into a vale, into a village veiled, Calzadilla de la Cueza. Near 9 p.m., time pressed for finding food and shelter. No need to fear in this town though. Calzadilla provides the best of both for a desperate man with little money. I am in no condition to judge quality truthfully, as hunger does make the best sauce. Anything offered, this ravenous scarecrow accepted gratefully, including allergenic bread. Even when the meat arrived with mushrooms, I merely push the fungi aside. Tomorrow, I'll be jet propelled through Spain. Indigestion will suggest a heart attack. Of course, I'll never know for sure if my pack isn't one pound too heavy or my pace a split second too quick. Thrombosis or indigestion? That's a question for tomorrow.

24/10/07

An odd sight seen yesterday: the third small migrating flock of sheep. Each flock, with lonely herder, seems more out of place and time than I do. Worse than pilgrims, they appear to wander the roads, with nowhere to go. Though Ireland holds a zillion sheep, I have never seen flocks like these.

Something odder, a bar connected to a gas station (or vice versa) makes a very bad combination, one that should not belong anywhere.

- - - - -

I've decided to give back my stolen march. Ain't that decent of me? Life treats me too well in this albergue not to take full advantage. After sleeping in, breakfasting, laundering and lunching, I perceive pilgrims passing I passed in Carrion yesterday. But, well rested, I prepare to hike hard now, in dry boots.

"Didja say dry boots?" God interjects. "Look at the clouds just whipped up for you, you lazy lummox!"

- - - - -

So, my pack-cover refitted, I strapped my brelly to my side, ever ready to defend myself at a moment's notice. Did it rain? No. All day God played with me. I never did get wet, but my unsuspecting lip got sunburned on a cloudy day, as my Blistex sits back in France.

The real divine game did not begin 'til dusk though...

Quick-stepping after late starting, I took Sahagun by 5:00 p.m., hitting the target set, and still not wet. Walking two more hours of daylight would carry my feet right off one map and onto another. Informed that two albergues waited within easy reach, 5 and 8 k away, I also heard warning of an alternate way. I decided to take the older, safer way, winding through every hamlet en route to Leon City.

Having time, I whiled a while in Sahagun. The civic past renders impressive the present. The ruins of Benedictine abbeys—straight from Cluny—include the current municipal albergue, staffed by a uniformed policeman. An authentic-looking Irish pub rules a nearby corner, without a Mick about, reminding me of another Irish mission. Without "one for the road," I hit the road, pounded pavement until at dusk I struck the expected fork and turn into Calzada for bed...

Never finding any available accommodation, I pushed through town to the dirt road beyond. With no desire to repeat last night's experience, I intended to stop in the next town, 3 km away, regardless. That's what I'd decided, and that's where this story turns weird...

Before any reader suggests that I've just been walking too long alone, or have done a half-gainer with full twist off the back of "the wagon," or have resorted to peculiar painkillers, let me assure you that none of the following originated in my imagination. Had any of you been walking with me, you would have seen the exact same, as plain as day.

Turning into Calzada, I saw two banks of clouds collect and collide from two directions to form on the horizon an arrowhead pointing at the path not taken. This display only pushed me in search of shelter. None evident, I viewed at the far end of town the setting sun send a fiery red column into the dark clouds. The pillar of fire that guided Israel did come to mind. Though this column led to the new route, I continued on the old one as determined.

Inside the point where the churning clouds met, a hand reached out. Just vapor or smoke, it looked exactly like a left hand held up to signal "stop."

The right hand must have been busy pulling from the clouds the clearest sky-writing letters I have ever seen. One letter at a time, the last letter first: "T- S (reversed)-I"... As "S" looked to emerge next, I guessed aloud "desist." Nothing more formed. "If you're talking to me," I opined, "S-T-O-P would better serve." As a lapsed Catholic, I really should have accepted the more precise Latin-based word.

At this juncture, I held up to haul out my map, while

twilight still allowed reading it. Surprising as it may seem, the map sided with God. The official billboard must have marked the older route in a dotted line (unexpectedly) and shown the alternate as a solid line. In another first, the old route avoided towns.

I'd chosen wisely but wrongly. Choosing too far back for turning, I stowed my map and marched on.

As if the warning appeared not dire enough, the dark cloud above the chosen path swirled to form one huge ugly hag aboard a broomstick. Her tattered cloak flew wide and wild as her familiar formed: a great slobbering hound from hell.

After that, I stopped looking skyward but recalled that a massive Alsatian had guarded the entrance to this trail. My staff I readied unnecessarily as that lurking beast allowed passage without a growl. Miles later, and darker, hope rose at the sight of a dwelling, only to dash on warning signs. The guards mentioned began to bark. One continued baying all the while I walked a mile. About a half mile farther, in a shady hollow I found a peregrino rest area, with an emergency shelter in shambles. "Better than nothing."

A witch's moon in a clear sky lit the grove. Picnic tables might stay dry. Maybe this would do. However, the trail also continued very visibly and, before descending into this depression, had revealed one distant light. "Just climb to that ridge," I urged my weary legs. "See what can be seen from there, before bedding down here." My climb rewarded me with two lights, but I turned towards the nearer and cheaper grove. That's when I heard, from the trees, the same baying for blood heard earlier.

Clever readers may guess my next move. I'll not say I ran towards the light. You could call it a dogtrot. I call it loping and hoping: hoping the hound would stay sniffing around the trees and shelter; hoping lights ahead promised more than another barn and another guard dog. Mostly I hoped my legs would hold up, and that I wouldn't fall down whenever I looked back.

Damn, a barn it was, with a wide-awake Alsatian waiting… but beyond the barn a village slept.

Another Calzadilla?!

The sole lighted doorway grabbed my eyes but offered me no albergue sign. Down the street another Alsatian watched and waited outside his gate. I returned to the light but only found a restaurant whose owner pointed me down the street to the hostel (just past the dog). Though the hour neared 9:00, the woman promised to stay open if I hurried back (past the dog). In the street, I discovered the dog had waited for his owner, who now chatted with him. Slipping past, I found the refuge unattended but open. Returning again to the street, I discerned the dog locked inside his gate. Unstymied, with one bark the clever beast brought a great black shaggy brute bounding from the shadows.

Bolting back to the door, I saw the blackguard abruptly turn left, as though never interested in my stringy legs. Hoping myself for a better meal than myself, I reached the restaurant as it emptied. Cold shoulder I expected but found instead a warm welcome and the finest peregrino menu to date. My choice (soup, chicken, and lemon mousse) took me on a trip to Paris and back, for €8.00. Superb!

Thurs. 25/10/07

Returned late from the restaurant, with washing and writing to do, I lay my sleeping bag on a bench outside the dorm room. Consideration came to naught as drunks arrived as I drifted off. Banging on locked doors, they demanded entry. Let in, would they shut up and settle down? Hangovers seem nothing less than divine justice.

Despite early rising, starting slips slightly late, after a hot breakfast at that restaurant.

Hiker's Tip for this still chilly morning: I have already recommended wearing a rolled-up sweatshirt around the hips under a pack. Alternatively, dress only your arms and shoulders with a sweatshirt after hoisting your pack. Then when the day and your exertions warm your body, there's no need to halt, unload, disrobe, and reload.

- - - - -

On my way out of town, I needed to negotiate past a pair of Alsatians loose in the street, but not a single peregrino anywhere. Miles and hours were walked without seeing more than three persons along the route—hunters with guns and dogs (another bad combination). Exceeding the range of both required striding another mile.

More than those three hunt here though. Twenty kestrels wheel above newly plowed ground and deal in death for mice and moles. The devil owns this section of trail, and Death runs it for him. I wouldn't approach this route again in less than broad daylight, and then only to visit "An oasis in the desert, and an angel of God's mercy" [penned in her visitor's book]. From Calzadilla I will forge my own pilgrim path in future. Who better than I?

No wonder an alternative route is proffered and preferred. I lost a piece of my talisman clamshell from Ireland on this cursed stretch. I did not turn back to look for it. I do not know the meaning of this sign for me and mine. I'm not guessing what any of the signs mean. I don't know more than I am telling; I refuse to tell more than I know. What happened did happen as written. I certainly don't know what any of the signs means to you. Beyond faith, I have empirical evidence that some conscious power tracks me, an ordinary guy. I'm relieved to note that this power does seem surprisingly benevolent, not hostile.

Generally, guidebooks recommend traveling with someone else, for safety and company. Travel books offer even more activities and distractions than our ordinary lives. I recommend traveling alone, to see whom you find. What you do with your discovery is up to you. I wouldn't ignore it however. Whatever you do, be consistent and true.

- - - - -

I can't believe I've only been walking six hours today. My watch says so; my psyche says no. Finally returning to the main route at Apeadero meant running one last gauntlet. Someone repeatedly fired shotguns by the trail. Most likely only an air-cannon for frightening birds, it surely scared me.

5:00 p.m.

Even six hours on that route proved too long. The other way is surely shorter. I should have landed in Leon city by now, not Mansilla. Having declared Leon my destination, I refuse to yield, not to that diabolical diversion. For the first time, I am deliberately marching into certain night. At least the moon rises full, and lights will probably reach out a long way from a major city. Still, 20 km stays a long way, after a long day, to start walking in twilight.

Hiker's Tip: Being the first peregrino down a path ain't always good. In Spain there's a spider that, rather than construct webs, as any respectably industrious arachnid would, only lets go with silky streamers, from any available tree, post or weed, neck, nose or eyelash. Yek!

CHAPTER 4
Leon to Santiago and on to Ireland

26/10/07 Fri.

The Benedictine Convent in Leon I barely reached before benediction and vespers. That's already past curfew, but once I gained entry, the nuns didn't throw me out. I felt lucky to reach Leon at all, as I had reripped my ligaments just stepping over a narrow ditch.

A day's rest describes my plan for Leon, with a visit to a doctor and a dentist. I've learned, however, that Santiago stands even farther from here than I thought: a two week walk, according to the warden. It had better not be, not for me.

Even more disheartening, a stabbing pain jabbed my ankle exiting the shower. Oddly though, my leg feels better for it, for now. Maybe that's a miracle for not cursing out loud in a convent. I never swore either when the nuns rang the 6 a.m. wake-up bell. I suspect some connective tissue in my leg ain't connecting anything anymore. Oh well...

- - - - -

Ever heard of tuna canned in vinegar, not brine or oil? Me neither. Can't eat vinegar. No big deal. Two cans of tuna are now donated to the convent. Better hurry if you want any.

27/10/07 Sat.

San Martin met me in the p.m., as planned this a.m.

For some distance after Calzadilla de la Cueza, a farmed valley between wooded hills reminds me of upstate New York. The impression doesn't last, as scenery soon reverts and then alters to an unkempt appearance unseen before. Approaching Sahagun, one enters a new administrative area, one with a bad history for organized agriculture. If graffiti can be believed, the entire district of Leon hates that past and the present pairing with Castile. Leon doesn't like Castile, or want to be like it. Land use and ownership seem entirely different. No mega co-ops operate here, with huge John Deere equipment plowing villagers into productivity.

I did not care overly for Leon City either. Some very nice set pieces inspire inside the old city's Roman walls. The cathedral's 2,000 square yards of stained glass can't help but catch your eye. I just prefer Burgos. She exudes more charm and class, though Leon boasts larger, older, busier.

- - - - -

Forget about that contest. The new winner, Astorga, offers a Roman and medieval citadel on a hill. It possesses an excellent albergue (where I mean to stay next time) and a chocolate museum, among others. A pleasant park nests atop the fortress, beside a grand square of stylish shops and eateries. I could swear too that the women here look better than elsewhere in Spain, due possibly to the Roman influence. I'll need to stay longer next time to confirm my thesis.

For now, I've stayed too long already. Shadows stretch. I should be past here if I'm ever to reach Galicia, where Santiago sits. I'm sick of looking at a map of Castile-Leon.

As pilgrim and tourist, I feel obligated to visit every major church and historic site along El Camino. However, sterling hiking brought me to Astorga from San Martin before 2:00, and I should not squander it scribbling here.

- - - - -

I arrived at the edge of El Ganza, at the edge of local maps, at the edge of darkness. The hostel, finally found (in a hamlet of fourteen souls), feels full of light, due to the couple running it. Informed of my allergy to bread and pasta, they presented me with a homegrown melon of unknown variety. I do know it tasted better than any I ever tried. My conscience won't allow me to steal a second slice from a melon that divine.

Being the sole male guest makes for a pleasant change too.

28/10/07, Sun.

Walking all day Friday, I sighted only one other pilgrim. Sailing away yesterday from Leon in the afternoon netted a catch of zero in six hours.

Morning comes cold in this region of Spain, in this season. Not all albergues offer heating either, or hot water. Anyone for a sack race (i.e., sleeping bags) to Santiago? Next time I mean to set foot in Spain by October 1st. I won't mail my gloves to Santiago either. At 8:30 a.m. the moon still lights the trail, aided by her unborn sun but helped more by Earth's sparkling frost. I should do warm-up exercises, bent knee sit-ups perhaps. Stretching would prove counterproductive in my current state. The most difficult decision on these mornings involves when to pull my hands from my pockets to blow my nose. That dilemma you will need to judge for yourself.

Starting with little water, I approached the next village, Hospital de Orbigo, gratefully. I'd have appreciated it anyway, as its history of supporting pilgrims lives on in the present. Medieval arches span the river that shields the town and a historic (and current) jousting yard of an order of crusading knights (not the Templars). The Knights of Malta, or Hospitalers of St. John, I always liked better than their rivals, whose towers still dominate El Camino. I know which side I would have cheered in the joust, though the Templars would more likely have won.

History says Templars lost in the long run, due to martial arrogance and prideful heresy. They lost the Holy Land and with that their special position in Europe. Papacy and royalty combined to suppress an order grown too rich and powerful for either to tolerate, or to manage on their own. Having established heavily endowed chapters throughout Christendom, after plundering the Middle East for centuries, the Templars had become the first international bankers, the partners of popes and kings.

Needless to say, no one that rich and powerful ever really loses. They remain the bankers behind the throne. An elitist secret brotherhood with their own religion and agenda, they're now called Masons or, if elite enough, Knights Templar still. Sometimes they go by other names: Illuminati, Bilderberg Group, Committee of 300, and occasionally, Congressional Committee. The white male rich elite that rules us becomes daily more wealthy and powerful.

They are no friend of pope or king (no wonder) as the American Revolution proves. They are no friend of democracy or freedom, as the American Revolution proves. Look around you.

- - - - -

Yesterday, two to four good parallel paths led in and out of San Catalina. Immediately after, the unsuspecting peregrino is slapped with the worst stretch in the entire route. I feel blessed for not having come onto it on a dark rainy night. With no path at all provided at one point, just the road (at a bad bend) leads on to paradise or perdition, or to Santiago. I guess government grants have gone awry. Something smells mighty Masonic here.

- - - - -

I should fittingly have finished today in a Templar stronghold, Pontferrada. Their castle, and museum nearby, impress or oppress. Moreover, my Mex-Oz pal, Jose, dawdles here, pleasantly surprised to see me but concerned that I overdo. He insists that I cannot reach the next hostel after sightseeing too long here. However, too much daylight remains to dally longer amongst the Templars.

I really do feel uncomfortable here anyway. Hitler's Nazis were right to consider themselves the new crusaders. Their chauvinist ideology, their quasi-religious militarism, even actual bloodlines, make the Nazis direct descendants of Templar and Teutonic Knights.

I push on to Cacabelos, ready or not.

NOT 29/10/07

[After one derogatory comment about the Masons, the next page of my journal disappears, with an account of my favorite stretch of El Camino. I never guessed "them" to be that powerful. However, my memory has not been robbed of that day.]

The day dawned in Cacabelos, on the best albergue of the French Route. In a churchyard, the unique modern construction suggests monk cells and cloisters of old. Well worth another long stumble in the dark to reach it, Cacabelos repaid this pilgrim in full.

From the valley where Cacabelos rests, I marched to O'Cebreiro on the mountain peak that divides Bierzo Province from Galicia. Though not my longest, that trek headed mostly uphill and finished at my long-time goal, the final province. The climb includes the prettiest countryside of the Camino, along an ancient cattle trail. Magical.

The small city of Villafranca also poses very prettily. A dozen pleasant Villafranca decorate the continent. I never met one I didn't like. Go to the Frankish city directly from Cacabelos; ignore the lengthy detour to Pieros. Another picturesque rural village, this one offers nothing unique. No way pilgrims of old would have gone out of their way.

I'm glad to have gone that way though. Otherwise, I would not have met and helped another Korean couple, young folk in need of aspirin and anti-inflammatory cream. They told me of my fame among Koreans on the trail and insisted on having their picture taken with "Fast Michael." According to their report, Pearl does poorly. May smiles return to that lucent face.

After pausing in the impressive churches of Villafranca, I pressed on quickly for Galicia.

Near the end of the day, where the climb grew steepest, I came closest to not continuing. I noted ahead of me a flock of sheep being guided up a path confluent with mine. Didya ever follow a flock of sheep up a dusty steep path? Not pleasant. Employing my staff to great effect, I bent hard into the mountain and pushed to the fork, just before the flock, where I used the stick to still greater effect. However, having bested the dog-driven herd, I could not rest on my laurels. In the thin air I panted to keep ahead of the crazy critters behind me.

Coming to the next village, still in the lead, I found the sheep continued up the main street on my heels. Maybe the muttonheads now looked on me as leader, but I saw a man approaching (down a side street) who looked possessive, but slow. I signaled to him a query about turning his flock. He shouted something incomprehensible to me, which the dogs at the back, and the sheep at the front, took badly. In a split second a wooly wave became a rushing torrent, capable of knocking me down, and dragging me under. I leapt into a doorway as the bleating fleeting flood swept past. I had not expected a sheep stampede, nor the shepherd at fault faulting me. Ill-will made me all the more anxious to reach the next town, O'Cebreiro, in Galicia.

Even in the dark, in a heavy mist, I located a fine hostel and a finer hostelry. For comfort and camaraderie, O'Cebriero supplied my best night on El Camino.

30/10/07

In the final province finally, I like it best, not just because it's last, but for its Celtic past. I also enjoy immensely passing markers with distances painted blood red, every half kilometer. All point downhill. Only dogs hold me back. A defending right hand swells like it's been bitten, but hasn't—but not for lack of trying. Two stray rottweilers repeatedly allow a fellow pilgrim to go unmolested. When, however, I eyed a scene too beautifully bucolic not to peacefully pause [doe-skinned Bambi-eyed bovines milked in an open barn], a hidden guard snarled as he leapt. Leaving me time to jump back, he left himself hanging mid-air on the end of his chain. I hope that hurt him, because my ankle feels bitten anyway. My jump just bit into my older injury.

71

In the next village, I thought about seeking medical attention, but only found two more examples of a particularly savage local breed. Part Alsatian and part Satan, they are not usually allowed off a chain, in a country that loves loose canines. Pausing to admire an ancient rough-stone chapel, I heard toenails on pavement behind me. Without looking back, I bolted through the churchyard gate and slammed it in the teeth of two devils.

My quick action should have saved my legs. Again, it didn't. The pain shooting up my Achilles bites as fiercely as the hounds of hell. The dogs corner me in a very interesting spot for an Irishman though, as I feel many of our own ruins must once have looked like this church.

Before the demon dogs lift their siege, to attack other pilgrims, I'll have time to note down the pains of some pilgrims already noticed. A Portuguese Englishman met last night has a cyst in his back. Despite doctor's orders to rest a month, he continues after a week. An Aussie sheila with a backache can blame infected kidneys, due to dehydration, dodgy water and pack pounding. Who do we know who might be similarly plagued?

Two women, of the tattooed and pierced tribe, were turned away from a convent refuge, possibly for rejecting the previous bug-infested hostel. Spewing unholy invective, they may well be witches, which the nuns feared, but they treated me nicely, sharing a local delicacy. In Spain, everyone collects chestnuts that fall by the million.

> "Chestnuts boiling on an open range
> by females looking slightly strange."

- - - - -

Escaping the graveyard and morbid thoughts, I allowed another Alsatian to delay me only slightly as he sunned himself in the middle of the road. Once past, I paused to pen this note, and let three more dogs harass me. A chain held the mad one, thank God. Generally dogs treat pilgrims casually, sensing our transience. Just don't stop.

Never mind German shepherds, German hikers nip at my heels now.

- - - - -

The Germans who appeared from nowhere disappeared. They must have stopped at the mountain cantina I pelted past. About 6 quick kilometers later, I stop to gather chestnuts in a roadside rest area. A car pulls up to produce an angry nut, a young man accusing me of stealing!

Attempting to remain calm, not hotly defensive or offensive, I offer the chestnuts to him. Some minutes of broken communication stumbled by in fractured English/ Spanish/French before I realized I'd been accused of running from the cantina without paying my tab.

Possibly this man's outrage merely hides a scam for bilking pilgrims. I laughed at the angrily waved bill (not the proper response). Then, I carefully communicated my seriousness about not paying debts I don't owe. I stuck to my guns, but only had a stick. I'd have been more worried had I noticed the attack dog behind me.

The bill server only threatened me with surveillance video and nearby police before departing. The police dog he'd left behind (not his after all) wandered off. Did the waiter not wait because he believed the beast with me? Was I saved by a stray dog? The most entertaining part of this farce came when I realized, halfway into protesting my innocence, that I was not entirely innocent. Bad cosmic timing. No, I never stiffed any café. However, last night I had promised a donation to the refuge but needed change. I meant to drop it in the box this morning. After God's wee reminder, I'll have to go back. Next time.

- - - - -

The 122.5 km marker stands in a rather special spot, as did a special dog, one double the biggest Alsatian met. I don't know the breed that produces monsters as big as yearling heifers, to herd the local big-horned cattle. Standing on all fours, this brute calmly looked me in the eye from an open gate. Thank God his owner came out from behind him, en route to her pasture.

Two km on, a herd of Holsteins was driven onto me. This familiar breed of cattle have horns docked here, like at home. I only recently recognized Holstein-Friesian's bad rep for dirty work with short horns. Recalling their nasty habit of tossing big heads on long necks, this old farmboy had worked through the whole herd without spooking one heifer, or being spooked, until encountering the only cow with horns in this herd. I could see Bossie thinking about employing her horns. Then a dog shot forward, to tend to the cow (not to me). Phew!

More unleashed Alsatians patrol Galicia than Alsace, Lorraine, and Germany combined.

- - - - -

In the village below, a magnificent *grandpere* chestnut stands, reminding me to put down a ditty cobbled together over a few days. If you don't recognize the tune straight away, I pity your callow youth. Pilgrims of old wrote popular ballads; this is my personal pilgrim anthem:

Santiago in the Morning

Nothing would better go
Than me with Santiago in the m-o-r-ning.
Nothing would raise a hymn
Quite like St. Jim when I greet him in the m-o-r-ning.
Where the divine glories
Twine around the door,
Whispering holy stories
I'd like to hear once more.

Limping in with pilgrims
When the frost is pretty and grim in the m-o-r-ning.
Chestnut burrs don't flutter down
So boy you better watch your crown, col-lect-ing.
If I had a miracle for only one day,
I'd pray a prayer, and here's what I'd say,
I'd say, nothing would better go
Than me with Santiago in the mo-r-ning, in the mo-r-ning.

- - - - -

A little ceremony I had planned for the 100 km marker. Unluckily, the slab hid in the dark. How dark? Glad you asked. Not even a star offered encouragement on a trail through trees. I couldn't see the hand in front of my face, a hand held up to keep branches from poking my eyes. If I stepped in shit, I didn't give a shit. When the feet started splashing, I took to a narrow ridge my stick found above the path. When I slipped, I feared a three-foot fall but found only three inches, as the path had crept back up in the dark. And my night vision remains better than most folks'!

Light near the 99.5 km marker allowed me to see the snarling dogs following me. One huge hound I'd talked my way by when a yappy ankle-biter got loose to prove his guard-dog status. Then the big fellow had to follow suit (always the way). Say, anyone see an arrow recently?

The nearest albergue to the 100 km marker stands 2 km away at 98 km.

31/10/07

Though fifty-three (and feeling older) I covered 53 km yesterday and still feel disappointed, as much of the distance ran downhill, and I pushed pretty hard all day. Not bad, just the same, for an old man with a gimpy leg, a gyppy gut, and gawky eyes. Don't forget a heavy broken pack besides. I seem to have developed a problem with the plumbing too. Probably dehydration. Must drink more today, but the water I drank yesterday might provide part of my difficulty.

Halloween could present another problem for me today. I'm a wee bit nervous about unknown local folk customs. Do pranksters paint yellow arrows to point pilgrims astray? Just for laughs? Just for badness? Halloween's a Celtic celebration, and we're too fond of pranking.

I fear in Ireland no similar trail, however sacred, would remain sacrosanct.

- - - - -

Injury #7: Today, stepping out from the first halt of the day, I felt a groin muscle pull in my left leg. Witnessing loads of single magpies over the last two days ("two for joy, one for sorrow"), I'm not seeing a single Alsatian though, or packs of them. One wolfish creature did emerge from a factory door, but on a chain unable to reach me—as well Fido knew.

- - - - -

2:00, I encountered the first Alsatian of the day. What's up with that? On the first day in Galicia, "border guards" number in the hundreds. Hostels and cafes send big mutts to welcome guests. Perhaps they're a test, to weed out weak pilgrims. Well, they didn't stop me. With luck, I'll arrive in Santiago on All Souls Day, a holy day of obligation, if I don't stay scribbling here.

Let me add, though I put myself through hell, Galician countryside looks like heaven. Ireland wishes its hills and valleys appeared this green and pleasant in November. Real cow paths form much of El Camino in Galicia. Hooves and pilgrim feet have trod here for centuries. Rough fieldstone, the favored construction material for walls, homes, and barns, can also roof here, but thatch too is traditional. Folk music sounds very Irish as well, and sometimes is.

Villages coming down the mountains into Galicia remain quite picturesque, as long as you don't look down. If you don't look, however, you will step in what you smell.

- - - - -

Portomarin provides another pleasing place for me. I do suspect, however, as I draw near my destination, that a swamp leading to a hole would look good if graced by a sign saying *Santiago*. Objectively, Portomarin does contain some unique features, e.g., a fortress church like in Croatia. A striking bridge and stairs lead to it and to good shops near a handsome square.

5:58 p.m.

The 55 km "milestone" marks the highpoint of the day. Running into darkness before attaining my target yesterday felt like failure to keep on top of time and distance. Today, I impressed me by getting ahead of schedule, through hard running—with pack, boots, bag and brelly.

Then, to put me behind only takes my behind. One messy pit stop put me ten minutes late. Not just gastro diffs delay me. First I must prove customer status to barmen though I don't drink (hard or soft drinks) or eat bread. Often kitchens have closed. The last overpriced ice cream bar in the bar I bought today. Consuming that slowed me too. Yet I hit the 55 km mark on schedule, with two minutes to spare. I knew then I could strike the 50 km stone today, and Santiago tomorrow.

Hiker's Tip: No better reward than an orange, if on the edge of your envelope—with one hour to go.

- - - - -

I meant to perform a wee ceremony before dark at the 50 km marker. A black rock picked off the trail would represent all despairing thoughts; a polished chestnut would portray hope. However, I never did reach that goal. I did do the distance, but the city of Melide intervened. Looking for the marker, and an albergue, added unwanted miles before my grim determination located the 50.5 km stone on the far side of town...Tomorrow it is then.

I should mention feeling pretty shitty today. Something has turned my stool to black soup. Maybe it's blood, because of the aspirin. That would cause still more dehydration. Just what I need! I had better get to sleep now. Tomorrow, I shall sleep the sleep of the justified.

01/11/07

Just after 8:00 a.m., and I have been out an hour. Yes, I thought that would impress you. OK, ya bastard, I was one minute late leaving the hostel and have not even finished the first 5 km. However, I have eaten breakfast and repacked my gear. I still departed before the first glimmer of daylight. Darkness held on too deep to see the path, never mind arrows or markers.

I would feel happy with my strong start, confident I could run, if I didn't have the runs and feel lightheaded. Oh well, I better get a move on if I'm to see Santiago today, or ever.

A solemn ceremony I did conduct at the 50 km marker. It felt nicely fitting. Some pilgrims apparently hold rites at every marker or large rock in Spain. How do they ever reach Santiago?

- - - - -

Ever been afraid to fart? Then you know. Yet, even with the early start, I managed to hold on until locating an open café with loo. I disapprove of peregrinos dropping pants, piles and paper all over the countryside. You'd be surprised where piles appear sometimes.

- - - - -

Here's another weird coincidence. Passing a pilgrim from England reminded me of another one passed recently, memorable for a forked hazel staff like mine. Though her compatriot employs an aluminum pole, that staff is also of hazel, as this pilgrim is named Hazel.

Hazelwood diviners use, maybe for divining divinity in humanity.

- - - - -

With every ache in my left leg, heel to groin, answering present, I'm doing the best I can to push myself with Irish martial songs. Recalled today: "The Ballad of Henry Joy

McCracken." Henry was one of the Presbyterian leaders of the 1798 rebellion. I've been in his old church on Rosemary St. in Belfast. His birthplace sits nearby. He was hung a block away in Cornmarket Square, near the courthouse where he faced sentence. The song means most to me because of the big rebel who used to sing it. God keep him.

"An Ulsterman I am proud to be..."

My fame extends beyond Koreans. Among Canadians, by cellphone a story precedes me up the path, about a mad Irishman who runs El Camino pell-mell, in full kit, while singing. I just met a Canuck, with her Brazilian canoodling companion, and they expected me. I did not reply: a story also circulates about a Canadienne and her Brazilian beau. I stuck to the story told all Canadians, about almost being Canadian, because when I was little my mother left me by the roadside in Quebec, near a famous shrine. Like Jesus at the temple, Mikey was left at the toilet.

- - - - -

Despite an unnecessarily long stop-of-necessity today, I came less than 1 km short (8 min.) at my mid-schedule break. I'd allowed for an hour break, but having met nothing of interest, I'm cutting that back, putting myself ahead of schedule. The truth is, I'm afraid to halt for long, for fear of muscles seizing and tearing. Looks like I will make Santiago long before dark. I'd better finish today, as I wouldn't bet on my ability to walk tomorrow. I still carry too much weight, but not on my skeletal body. Fat cells, said never to go away, sure do hide well on me.

Let me count some blessings, as I have recorded each ache. I am amazed at never falling to the flu, cold or hives throughout my journey. I've not known a good night's rest for a month. Meeting and greeting new folks daily from around the world (plus new insects and littler bugs), I've slept in overcrowded rooms (and on airplanes) with them. I've been meeting new food-handlers too, directly and indirectly, plus new foods. I've been walking from the hot and sweaty into the cold and wet, and back again. I've drunk foreign water and breathed strange pollen and dust. Yet I have scarcely sneezed once. God bless me indeed.

After the 11 km stone, markers disappear! Arrows grow scarce. Above Santiago though, a huge hostel collects incoming pilgrims. Should I stop? Not on your life. Having come this far, I am tramping in to the cathedral. Boots, pack, staff and hat will come with me, for the final 3 km.

At the official "Santiago" road sign, I pause to touch it with my pilgrim staff, bound with the rosary from a St. James Church in Bosnia, a souvenir of Medugorje promised to a niece.

It's official: I have walked from France, 800 km away, without being passed by one pilgrim. No hiker ever seen before me went unpassed. I know of no one starting after me who finished before my beat-up body. I wasn't racing anyone except an econo-airline, and I think I've won.

Seven hundred fifty klicks in three weeks, including one week off (for injury, laundry, and tourism), ain't bad. My handicaps actually added miles besides. The final segment (307 mountainous kilometers), allegedly two weeks work, got done in under one—the last 250 completed in five days of dysentery by a limping, sleep-deprived, allergy sufferer. Fifty kilometers per day under a brutal pack I call fairly clipping (even for a young man). All the while this diary duty demanded doing. I repeat, "Not bad."

You might say miraculous, and you might be right.

By the bye, I played five games of chess en route. Lost zero, and I'm not good.

- - - - -

I'm ready now. Exhausted, with 2 km to go, I'm ready to swing in, singing, to the cathedral. I will bring to Santiago all the songs that brought me here, though some seem less than appropriate to pilgrimage. I'll save for the cathedral square "O Sacred Head Surrounded." All who hear me may think me mad, and they won't be far wrong.

More miracles. Call it coincidence if you like. All the way here, tromping through heaven and hell, I have been joking with other peregrinos, "This had better be one hell of a cathedral." Well, 'tis. Not worth running halfway while half crippled, as a rule, but I arrive on a holy day.

With no notion of Mass times, I hoped All Souls Day might offer an evening service. Pressing on all day, without halt, I did arrive before dark above the city. I also hoped to feel a fillip at the sight, but truly ran on empty by then. I expected to find a pedestrianized route directly to the cathedral. No such luck. The Way wound less clearly than ever. If not greeted personally, I expected large helpful signs to welcome and direct poor pitiful pilgrims. Nothing.

Disappointed but not disheartened, on and on I tread, until I located what I took to be the side door of the cathedral. Finding the door unlocked but no services on, I entered a side chapel open for eucharistic adoration. My pack unloaded, I laid my staff before the altar. Amen.

My private visit became a public rosary recital, making my Bosnian rosary even more appropriate. Two litanies and a benediction ensued before Mass began on the main altar, all prior to my finding food, water, shelter, public loo or pilgrim info. God has a wicked sense of humor.

From "tourist phones" I learned more about the duties expected of me. With less guidance than given to the holy hermit who found the grave of St. James, I located the same beneath the altar and his venerable effigy above. My staff and other objects already sacred to me have now touched holy ground. My duty done, I can now find a bed, maybe.

02/11/07

After quick queries and weary wandering, I gave up on finding an albergue in town in this season. Around the corner, a two-star pensione promised that famed guidebooks praised them. A single (en suite) with TV (Spanish) cost €25. Extremely reasonable, it seemed dear after €5.00 refuges. May I live to return to the Pensione Linares.

Ashamed to say, I zonked without showering. Waking at 6 a.m., I cleaned up and returned to bed. Glorious. This pensione turns out a godsend, ideally located for exploring the city today and for departure tomorrow. The albergue sought was a ghost. Still a mile away, the Seminary Minor finishes as a hostel after the holidays. I do recommend staying in Santiago if you can however. Any true pilgrim deserves to enjoy the city, a treasure, a well-earned reward.

El Officio del Camino, when found, treated me so poorly, it remains poorer a donation I'd have gladly given. I got my due anyway: a stamp in my peregrino passport, plus a *compostela*. My advice to pilgrims: know your due, and where to get it. The office operates across the plaza outside the opposite side door of the church, upstairs in the old residence for visiting bishops.

Workers in the organization supposedly dedicated to aiding pilgrims are prone to repeat, "A tourist expects; a pilgrim accepts." I agreed until finding out for myself that this mantra only excuses (not accuses) misconduct. Anybody, but a pilgrim particularly, should expect Christian care from people taking the job to provide it. Workers call themselves "volunteers" to suggest their work goes unremunerated. Generally, that's not so. Having advised pilgrims, I offer these words to workers: If you don't enjoy helping people in desperate need, get another job.

Incidentally, claiming to run a refuge should be illegal if your establishment fails to meet a code of standards posted plainly at the door (in Spanish, French, Italian, English and German), regulations designed to protect true pilgrims. Don't bother complaining about my complaining. I only state facts and am sworn to return to make better caminos for others, at my own expense. Today I doled out free Santiago cake and anti-inflammatory cream to fellow peregrinos.

I also doled out my favorite Irish rebel tune, to explain my rapid progress across Spain. "Kelly, the Boy from Killan" fairly bounced about Cathedral Square.

- - - - -

Some of those pilgrims entertained I met by chance that night, where they still partied in the plaza. The free wine offered could've plastered me, but I remain on the wagon. Perhaps my behavior suggests I enjoy a drink, but I really do not feel the need. Liberty cannot be bought in a bottle.

Before departing, three treasures of the trail I laid at the altar of St. James Victorious: a green oak leaf cockade from an Irish pilgrim's hat; a giant chestnut, seed of a greater Camino; a bright crystalline rock from the hard shining path.

3/11/07

The final odd coincidence: I left on the lope again, despite allowing plenty of time to reach the station. I timed the walk last night and checked the station layout. A quarter hour would do the trick. Very organized and responsible, no? No. I should have allowed a quarter hour just for squeezing out the pensione's three locked doors when a pack bulged on my back and bags filled my hands.

I would have missed the bus had I not checked ahead the number and location of the departure bay, or if the driver's watch had run one minute fast. My wallet would have missed the €54 bus ticket (to the French border). Thank God I had planned not to rush my crippled legs. Damned, I had to run regardless, but only through purgatory.

Arriving flustered, nearly flummoxed, I couldn't catch what the driver said about numbers on my ticket. I guessed he was pointing out my seat number, but I could not find that info on my stub or the seats. Sitting where I wanted—not too far back, nor too far from the luggage compartment—I didn't relax but grew more nervous about what the driver had said. What if he had directed a transfer? I decided, if an English-speaking passenger could be found, to enquire.

Turns out, I was right the first time, about seat numbers, which were written on the windows. Did I need to move? Nope. Out of sixty-two seats, I had seated myself correctly, in #43.

I did nearly miss a transfer though, due to a loo visit. Now I can see and concede that missing my bus in Ireland only provided a useful warning, one taken seriously. Missing the bus today would have cost me far more. Such a close escape! Luckily, I came from the loo, or I might have shit myself.

More irony: With my Camino over, I thought to leave hardship behind, for the comfort of civilization. So, on the first night away from Santiago, I get put out of a train station onto the cold streets while waiting for an early morning train. Another train I'd been told to catch the night before had never been a real possibility. Lacking my E.U. passport necessitated an easy end-run around the border checkpoint. That may have complicated matters.

To make matters worse, the shelter that I found had to be shared with a fellow backpacker who also carried a huge case of the flu. Doomed. At least he played chess.

Worse yet, when finally allowed to entrain, I had another plague follow me on board: two yahoos promptly turned on cellular radios.

- - - - -

Well, I won't be on board long and need to stay awake for exiting at Biarritz. From there I'll fly tomorrow. My Camino will be over. Despite the litany of pain listed previously, I would like to say that I completed a good Camino. "*Buen camino*" is the common parting phrase for peregrinos, but a good camino is uncommon among first-timers, especially those who (a) have not read up, (b) do not speak Spanish, (c) are not Australian.

After my own experience, I no longer doubt the original peregrino's story. The tale told by a loony hermit about a guiding star works for me. What remains below the high altar of the Cathedral Santiago could be Santiago. Does that mean Christ reigns above that altar? Maybe.

I do know this: many scientific theories get based on less evidence than I personally experience of a conscious benevolent force, looking out for me. That remains a theory though.

As any Christian knows, that ain't good enough for God. **So, my final tip for pilgrims is this:** If you have your faith, protect it from reason and pride (and particularly from the Jesuits). Massive anecdotal evidence exists for the existence of God, and no proof for the opposite. Moreover, people being born pre-programmed to believe in God is scientifically proven, as is living longer and happier if in compliance. Disbelief is not an easy option. Doubt does not free us from all strictures of belief. If no Being reigns above us, we move to the top, meaning every action requires greater concern and consideration. Consistency grows paramount if an individual is to create, not destroy, himself. More care, not less, we require if no God lives to forgive us.

You who do believe must take care not to be prideful, over-confident or self-righteous. You can put off others, off their faith. For your sin, you may yet be punished with dark despair.

As I write these words, I may be a dead man walking, as according to the doctor I should not be walking, never mind flying.

Oh, my passport did wait patiently for me in Biarritz. Ireland or heaven, here we come!

10:00 a.m. 10/11/07

Precisely one month from beginning my Camino, I walk again in Ireland, to my personal Finisterre (End of the Earth): Bantry, Co. Cork. I ought to rest my legs as promised, but I have only one stretch left to complete my circuit of Ireland on foot. Of course, by rights I should have carried on to the Spanish coast. However, since Ireland has prior claim, and I can claim prior ignorance of the epilogue Espagnole, my crippled legs are obliged to finish Ireland first. Besides, as I'm already obligated to repeat a doubled Camino, I would prefer to add a few days of new scenery to the far end.

Of course, the flu I had managed miraculously to avoid in Spain caught me in Ireland. Though the day goes gray and overcast, I do not blame Irish weather. Indeed, a better day for hiking could not have been expected in June, never mind November. No, I must blame France again, for closing a train station on a cold night. Whatever, Ireland now has one more fast-flowing stream. I also endure a chesty cough and headache, despite aspirin taken for my inflamed leg. Yet my troubles are as nothing, though I did feel sorry for myself until witnessing the trials of a fellow passenger on the bus to Cork last night.

In Dublin, to check out visa applications at the Russian embassy, among other things, I only arrived in time for the final coach to Cork through very quick and clever use of public transport. Others arrived even after me, though they only came from a nearby pub.

They were soon sorrier than I. Buses in Ireland provide no toilets. On this particular express service, coaches are legally forbidden to stop in spots not designated. In former days buses would regularly pull over anywhere to turn the ditch into a urinal. One big fella onboard, with a small bladder, badly missed the good old days.

Several times he paced the aisle, beseeching the driver to stop. He sat cross-legged an hour, until a town's traffic made the bus stationary. Then his female friend begged to be let off, successfully. Turning to report that to him, I discovered the news had come too late. Not wanting to move now, until he knew everyone else knew, the poor chap belatedly fled the bus. His friend managed to reboard before the bus left town, but the driver waited for nobody.

Overheard cellphone talk told me that the pissed, pissed-on, pissed-off boy, stranded in a strange town, now assisted the police. See, I've no real problem. If you think you're having a piss poor day, pause and reflect.

Noon

My headache for now I can cure just by escaping Cork City and "civilization." Finding a civilized route to Kinsale seems impossible though. No road grants room to pedestrians here. Someone did leave €20 on the road for me. That was very civilized.

- - - - -

I opt out on Kinsale. I can't take that busy road any more. The old direct route to Bantry proves more fitting, as my ancestors certainly came this way on foot more than once. Possibly the reverse route took them out of Ireland. Newer roads would shorten my journey, but leaving main roads provides amazing relief.

- - - - -

Once again, I have been marching through pitch darkness. With no light, I nearly continue in permanent darkness. Beware willow hedges. A few days' growth allows willow branches to reach for your eyes. Not blinded before Bandon, I stopped in a fine B & B on the far side of town.

11/11/07

Bandon to Dunmanway was the best I could do before darkness dragged me down. November cuts days short. I'm sure my predecessors could have stridden in summer from Shandon Bell to Bandon, and Bandon to Bantry. On a good horse, or better bike, they may have done it in a day, before the rise of cars. For a motorist, a few hours suffices, but on foot you spend hours pinned against hedges or searching futilely for alternative routes. Slightly suicidally, I pushed on in the dark, looking for a tourist hostel a few miles down the back road to Bantry.

Quite a few miles from Dunmanway, the hostel sits far up a narrow mountainous road, but I found it—closed.

12/11/07

Never one to say die, I discovered on the property a very stationary gypsy van. How fitting and old-fashioned! Able to open this, I spent a reasonably comfortable night.

Morning provided a *belle* view, only partially damaged by spruce farming. I hurried on my way, early enough to aid a real farmer. As he moved sheep with two dogs (one a young inexperienced pup), two rams broke for the road. Recalling an embarrassing encounter with Spanish sheep, I ran forward gallantly regardless...My pilgrim staff served nicely as shepherd's crook, possibly preventing a nasty accident. Thanked for my effort this time, I feel my farm-cred restored.

This route, generally not heavily trafficked, I think I could recommend, but I wouldn't recommend hiking around Ireland generally. Even if you do escape being added to the carnage along Ireland's highways, you'll never escape the garbage along them. Short of dying, there's no escaping the litter and wholesale household and industrial tipping.

Pushing back dark thoughts, I remind myself: if my legs survive one more day, I will complete another quest. Suddenly the road reminds me of an Irish relative who died in America a few years ago. From Johnstown, Co. Kilkenny, he became quite a pilgrim as an Irish bard and navvy.

Surprisingly, Co. Cork, arch-rival of all Kilkenny hurlers, reminds me of one. In desperate need, I come upon a cross-road shop with his same name above the door. In the window a poster advertises a nearby Irish music fest in Johnstown, Co. Cork. Above the shop Kilkenny's county colors fly as the local G.A.A. happens to hold those hues.

- - - - -

Along Irish byways holly bushes grow thick and fast. From these evergreens I plucked a sprig to decorate my pilgrim's hat. Wearing this green cockade and a pilgrim pouch, I ran the final mile on my damaged legs, mad man that I am. Landing in the town square, I had enough breath left to let loose one rebel song over Bantry Bay, for the men of '98.

From St. Brendan's boat there, this American ran to the ancestoral burial. For all souls left behind, many a rosary I said on younger knees. For them a rosary I bring today and holly, representing everlasting life and love. I do not leave the leaves but carry them away for a sister's final Christmas, and for a certain witch (not a sister) to whom I might mean more in future—if I have a future. She'll appreciate holly. To her I also give much credit for my success in Spain and Erin. This Damsel Dulcinea, whose favor I wear, I could not face with failure. Clever reader, you guess my final tip to all pilgrim souls.

I ran into Bantry not entirely for dramatic effect. A bus required catching. The bus passed as I bolted back from the cemetery, and didn't stop. Never mind, the next bus will still put me in Cork City in time. God gives me time to repair myself, to prepare for long rides with normal folks.

EPILOGUE
Ireland to America

You never know your luck. I'd been kicking myself for three days, walking to Bantry, for failing to leave unneeded belongings in the Cork bus station. If connections turned out tight (for returning to Shannon Airport), I'd want my pack handy. Instead, taking a chance, I left my luggage in the left-luggage of the hostel. Though certain to hike straight by the station, I didn't know for sure I could find lockers there. I did know the hostel offered no locker or any security.

Mea culpa, plain laziness left the pack behind. Passing the station, I found a baggage office, which forced me to reconsider. Recalling something valuable left in my pack, a $50 chess clock, memory directed me to a $10 chessboard once stolen in that very hostel—a warning surely. Still, stinginess left my pack in the free luggage room.

At the time I estimated the board to be of no value to a thief motivated simply by pleasure in doing evil. Though all else in my pack now amounted to little of monetary value to others, it remained valuable to me—and to evil.

Well, evil did not win this time. On my return, my pack sat unmolested. Moreover, if left in the station, my pack would have robbed me! Missing the earlier bus in Bantry meant missing the baggage office's open hours. Stuck in Cork, I'd have missed my flight to New York.

St. James' Church, Upstate N.Y., 18/11/07 Sunday

See where I have ended up? Here where my Jacobean pilgrimage began, I have returned with the same pilgrim staff and rosary, for a final blessing before bestowing them as vowed:

> Dear Maureen,
> At your wedding I did vow I would do, and I have done. May you ever say the same.
> What I have done is to deliver a rosary (on a pilgrim's staff) from St. James Church in miraculous Medugorje, Bosnia, to St. James Cathedral in Santiago, Spain, via this St. James, your parish church. Additionally, first and last, the rosary visited holy ground in Ireland, earth sacred to our family in Co. Clare and Co. Cork, completing the full circuit of Ireland with me.
> That circuit was entirely on foot, as was the pilgrim route from France to Santiago.
> What I have done is the hardest I ever did do.
> May you never say that about your marriage, even if it's true.
> Dia duit

As if 1,000 km is not enough, I have gone farther than my feet have tread. Prior to this pilgrimage, I had long since ceased to attend weekly Mass. I vow now to return. Somewhere, you may see me standing at the back. I'll be the man not going to communion. I'm too good a Catholic not to know that I'm not a good enough Catholic.

Though I remain a non-believer, I have reason to think the God I once knew is true. If so, I owe Him this respect and recognition. No reward do I expect. Faith, the prerequisite for that, I lack. I will live and die a skeptic. This far I can go. If empirical knowledge does not suffice, then pride remains my great sin. But Christ did have mercy on a doubting Thomas once.

I claim no epiphany on my pilgrimage. I'm not an epiphany kind of guy. If saddled up, I ride into Damascus, or the horse had better be dead (for his own sake). However, my whole experience is too much, the odd coincidences too many, the unexpected aid too timely, the instruction too obvious. I dare anyone. Engage in any great physical endeavor on your own, away from the common distractions of ordinary life. At the end, see if you still think you are alone.

BOOK 2

Pain to Spain

Between his first and second Camino, the author completed circling the Earth on earth, hiking wherever great or grand suggested, from the Grand Canyon in a day, to the Great Wall of China for a day, to the Great White Way in a day (Bronx/Yonks line to Battery), and including all of Ireland, of course. Next he backpacked across America, Florida to Canada, up the murderously, monstrously mountainous Appalachian Trail, before publishing a book, *A Voice in the Wilderness*. On the wildest journey of all, he traveled from agnostic to gnostic, to knowing God and knowing who looked for him to look for Him in Spain...

CHAPTER 1
America and Ireland to Italy and France

In the Air! Harroo-Hooray! Tues. 22–2-11

A new adventure begins, with unexpected ease due to the generosity of family and strangers. Sure, some last-minute rushing did occur, but none too madly. True, when into this quixotic quest your intrepid penman flew, he suffered the added handicap of heavy flu. Pain and doubt, more than turbulence, buffeted his flight. However, a certain sister had exuded a healing balm of calm. Pity she cannot claim the same of her brother. Chauffeured, fed and pampered, the poor pilgrim acquired a tent (on sale) and a borrowed guidebook due to his kind kin. Ah, to think this same sister was once rewarded for looking after her little brother by his stepping on her ingrown toenails.

Wait a minute! Sisterly altruism just morphed into bloody revenge. She helps me to perpetrate months of brutality to my own feet. She practically put me on the plane to pain! Of all the vicious, Machiavellian, twisted...

"Oh, treachery! Seek it out!"

I can still depend on the kindness of strangers. Even before Sis delivered me to purgatory, flight confirmation required consideration from a public servant with a phone.

Though that call cost the public naught, it saved this citizen much, and began his pilgrimage like he (and Christ) would like. The great misfortune in this exceptional good fortune lies in its exceptionalness. May God always aid all who help pilgrims.

[P.S.: Quite miraculously, I carried my pilgrim's staff straight through security and onto the plane—where a full row of seating I arranged for myself. No, I never used the stick to frighten anyone away.]

Wed. 23–2-11

Old Erin herself greeted me kindly with temperatures 25 degrees above frozen New York. Not that I'm complaining about the bright day February offered that city. To bemoan global warming and then whine about a nice crisp day in the Big Apple just won't do. Secondly, that very sort of day, bright white and deep blue, chilly and cheery, I often missed in milder, grayer Irish winters. Thirdly, experience teaches pilgrims never to complain about the weather, as God can always make that worse, and usually does.

Under overcast sky, Dublin Airport still impresses with its lively bustle, but the city depresses. Though New York is departed on this page, Old Dublin is dead. A grayness caused by economic depression, reminiscent of the black seventies, goes unassuaged now by any feeling of communality or common purpose. Officialdom touts a new multiculturalism, the same that leaders of Britain, France and Germany just dismissed as a failure.

I did not hesitate to patron a special Polish eatery and grocery myself, having been impressed by that culture's commitment to quality. I sincerely wish the Poles well and good luck with keeping Poland Polish.

Some nuggets of Old Dublin remain for mining. For a pilgrim of St. Jim, a Dublin Biddy in one of many Euro stores cut extra slack, the first stranger to act an angel on this pilgrimage. A fillip felt rises from kindness and respect revealed, more than from the cash. May angels lift her feet above the rough pavement of her native streets.

If you can't find something of interest on Parnell Square, you really should "Get on your bike." As the square offers a rack of bikes for rent, something suits even those not suited by anything else. The Garden of Remembrance, sacred to Irish Republicans, graces the square, as does the H.Q. of Sinn Fein (republicans who haven't forgotten). The Irish Writers Museum holds another corner while a thriving theatre nearby keeps alive the literature of Nobel winners and new talent. I enjoy another museum, the free Hugh Lane Gallery. A painting by Monet, "Concert in the Tuilleries," made me realize how much recordings and radio would come to cost community, even before TV, autos, and air-conditioning. The whole world would follow America down the one-way dead end of individualism.

I enjoyed even more sharing insights with museum staff, all true Dubliners. To the brave new worldly world all is not yet lost. In addition to its other treasures (paintings and people) the museum hides one of the many secret gardens that endear Dublin to me. Such retreats grow increasingly essential to my essence, an identity under attack.

Thurs. 24/2/11

Never fly with flu. After three flights, you might land in Insanity, not Italy. Some say the two states differ little. If landed in Italy, I intend to spend the night in the third airport of the day—thus crashing in Insanity after all. This airport rates as superior accommodation for a pilgrim (pellegrino) however. An immigration official, claiming to represent Italy, insanely waved me through when I tried to explain that my E.U. passport had just run out-of-date. Though I hold a perfectly good U.S. passport, I suspect that French authorities will take a less cavalier attitude toward travel documents. Never mind, walking on behalf of a higher authority, I check in first at the airport chapel, unapologetically Catholic in Italy. Secluded, but open all hours, this room appeals: a peaceful, pretty place—not too "busy" (with people or paraphernalia). A few restaurants remain open, even after midnight, in an airport abandoned now by most legit travelers. Quite a few folks seem to reside here though, making me more comfortable and uncomfortable simultaneously. Looky here: a vending machine for freshly baked pizza! Does that indicate Italy or Insanity? The airport name, "Malpensa," suggests "Thought bad." Such honesty does seem slightly insane.

Fri. 25/2/11

I've decided to stall a day in Milano, one of the great cities of the world. This fashion/financial capital deserves more than I can afford, in time or money. Besides, the airport offers a left-luggage. If you backpack anywhere, you know how precious and rare such facilities become in our insecure society. Leaving your pack somewhere safe feels akin to leaving prison. This backpacker will postpone the moment he must suit up. He already carries a chest full of phlegm, plus an eye sty. [No, not an "I-ti."] My shoes require a gradual start too. Purchasing them some time ago, I hesitated to wear the pair too much, for fear of wearing them down too much. Three thousand km I have to go in these, or break in new shoes midway. I can certainly postpone blisters and corns for now.

While revealing guilty secrets, I confess to dining in an Iti McDonalds already. Its strangeness, not its familiarity, appealed. Surprisingly different, it made me miss the genuine version, though not a fan of those.

Later and Late, Back at the Airport

Disgorged from the train station onto the lively streets of Milan, I inadvertently allowed a whoop to escape. Like a cowpoke hitting Dodge, or a culchie loose in Dublin, I wandered out, wide-eyed and bushy tailed. As from the station (not Centrale) a citadel can be spied, I accepted fate's suggestion for exploration. No tourist info office appeared to direct me otherwise. A fortress of red brick impresses if you have no cannon with you. As a museum, this structure remains undefeatable, except on a blue-hued darling day like this, by a city wielding so many sights. A sunlit stroll through cosmopolitan streets beats a dark castle, and few cities provide a principal promenade to match Milan's. From the imposing fortress gates, past the suitably striking equestrian Garabaldi, I stride down medieval streets to the Piazza Duomo, where the fantasia of a confectionary cathedral waits. The obligatory pause at this episcopal edifice only delays the onslaught of barbarians on the bastions of fashion beyond.

I don't know why I failed to enjoy the day more. Tired, I guess. The weather felt less pleasant than it looked. Oddly, traveling from NYC to Dublin to London to Milan, the farther south I went the colder the weather went, despite growing sunnier. Gray Dublin warmly embraced me with temps over 50 F., a good 20 degrees above Milan. Mostly my complaints rise from my aching feet. Using my head, I hiked all day without a backpack, but my feet still ache to the bone. My shoes do not live up to expectation. What can I do now?

My dawgs propose and second a motion: return early to the airport. Although made after nightfall (at 6:30 p.m.), this decision produces a short and discouraging day of hiking. I did accomplish an important task though. I got my long hair chopped a bit, exciting and expensive activity in a foreign country, where I command the language and the barber even less than usual.

Are you satisfied now, Ma? If I die on this odyssey, my corpse won't disgrace you. As hair does continue to grow on corpses, I'll do my best to die where someone will find my body quickly.

Sat. 26/2/11

I shift as slowly as I dare into top gear. Starting out in Milano struck me as appropriate, having passed that way once on pilgrimage to Rome from Ireland, not entirely on foot, but shadowing the medieval Route Francais. Remembering the multi-spired white cathedral, festooned with 5,000 statues outside, I found the interior calming by contrast (as intended by its builder/bishop, St. Charles Borremeo), and thought it a dramatic kick-off point. Two small statues I did locate inside: two St. Johns unusually paired, but not oddly. As the Baptist revealed Christ's coming, the Evangelist did so in his Gospel, plus a second coming in Revelation. One John would meet Mary as kin before Calvary; the other left Calvary as kin. Also family to the latter, brother James would become patron of pilgrims, while the first John (Baptist) would patron protectors of pilgrims: Knights of St. John Hospitaler, aka Knights of Malta—not to be confused with a rival crusading order: the Knights Templar.

After tramping across Milan and back, I entrained for Genoa, the city embossed at the top of Italy's boot where pilgrims face the final chance for choice: Rome or Santiago. Turning back is ever possible, and Christopher Columbus took the fourth course here. A Genoan, he sailed to Spain (recently freed of Moslems), since in the east the other sacred site of pilgrimage, Jerusalem, had been lost by Templars to Islam, and all hope for recapturing trade routes had fallen with Constantinople. Columbus sailed west to go east but hit America, from where I come to try the older way to Spain and Finisterre (the End of the Earth before Columbus). I march before the End-of-the-Earth-as-We-Know-It is brought about now by the Templars, who also sailed to America, to found the New Jerusalem, and who continue to engage in disastrous crusades plundering the Middle East.

Columbus took the easy choice, as the Maritime Alps fairly shove any wayfarer into the sea. Now, odd elevators in mountains make staying easier. I found hard leaving a place that so embraces travelers. Among enclosing streets, six separate locals aided this stranger. Most were paid to aid, but cash does not guarantee service—especially to foreigners.

Even more graciously, Genoa gifted a special Mass, in a compellingly graceful, grace-filled cathedral. Not a scheduled service, a wedding Mass this solitary pilgrim happily happened upon. In keeping with my vow to help other pilgrims, I donated to the priest's plate and to the bride as she starts her daunting journey. In return, I asked that she pray for another wife who helps a husband unable to help himself. I intercede myself for an unhelpful wife, as I need my own transgressions forgiven before starting afresh. Then I can pray for another couple, toward whose marriage I march. May they be better blessed (blessed by my presence at least).

Having granted all the time to Genoa I could, I boarded transport a final time, to the edge of greater Genoa, to a town whose name I already knew. Savona, N.Y., had grown on the edge of where I grew up. Old Savona might teach me the meaning of her name. Nope, departing disappointed, I only knew the new Savona bears no resemblance to the old, but I did trip upon a campground, one my map promised without revealing the route. Though seasonally closed, like all camps, Buggi Camp opened enough for me to pitch a tent and did not fulfill the threat of its unfortunate name.

Sun. 27/2/11 (No day of rest)

After a whole day hiking without a pack, I started yesterday without one but finished under pack, before breaking in my new tent. I'm pretty pleased with the day, my equipment, and the decisions made before facing my first full day of backpacking. My next decision discards pounds from my pack of course. As a sign of good faith, I leave at the campground a mini-Bible, a bandage, and a teabag for any other poor fool who passes this way.

Finding my legs willingly return to service, I decisively cut into the mountains rather than continue in and out along the narrow cluttered coast. Marching to the call of church bells and duty, I climb steeply to a steepled chapel, but arrive too late. Yesterday's service may need to serve as a vigil Mass. From the hill I spy snowy peaks. Marching at them, bootless feet will stay below the thick ermine capes, and high thin air, of these haughty barons.

"Dead-reckoning" doesn't bode well for a stranger in these parts, but locals who should know how to help, can't or won't, and the best map obtained still fails in the details. Carrying this much weight, I cannot afford many dead ends or other wrong guesses. My legs, not yet fully in gear, still do not disappoint, but I could use the service of a good eyes-ears-nose-and-throat man. Anybody know one who makes tent-calls on mountaintops in Italy?

My case would expand his expertise. Pressures of a tightly belted pack, and tighter wound brain, worsen my acid reflux. Acid does help cut the phlegm though. Hacking while hiking, p-tooey, I follow likely paths until they peter out, then employ my staff to hack through to another path, or to a road that may only prove too lethal to use. Then I go back to hacking, and repeat the recipe until exhausted.

I reach Altare the way Napoleon's army came, between the Alps and Apennines. One villager has English enough to warn me: turn back before a heavy snow falls. Though I'd only felt too hot today, I did not doubt him, but still pushed on to Mellare. First, I spent too much time and cash, buying any food served in bars open at 5:00 p.m. on Sunday in a mountain village. Fittingly, refreshingly, I visited a pilgrim chapel of San Rocco, who I never knew as a fellow pellegrino de San Giacomo, and the first among pilgrims. I must learn more about this saint, always depicted with wounded leg, and a hound, bearing bread. My experience with canines on the Camino suggests they might eat my leg, but never feed me. As for me eating a loaf from a dog's mouth, that would be miraculous.

I did, however, take dubious water from a bar's faucet, after leaving very "dubious water" in the loo, before heading uphill into the dusk in a doubtful direction. Still, the K-2 Restaurante, just over the first hump, stalled my progress again. This hostelry deserves the blessing of St. James and the custom of all pilgrims who pass this way.

Found in the dark, Mellare rewarded with a pallet-maker's open drying shed. Accepting the unintended offer graciously, carefully, I discerned two parallel pallet piles about ten feet high, half the height of other stacks. Up I clambered, out of the reach of guard dogs or weary watchmen. Far from frozen ground, I will not wake up shivering in a wet, snow-covered tent. I resolve to leave my fairly comfortable perch before daylight regardless.

Mon. 28/2/11

Good to go before 5 a.m., I felt foolishly relieved to discover just a dusting of snow, but abruptly, in the dark, white fluff began to fall like the fake stuff in a TV commercial hooked on continuous feed. The struggle with my pack-cover alone, under these conditions, grew Herculean. Then the road began to climb again. My map told me I'd avoided most peaks, until I realized: the name of the village targeted provides another Italian word for mountain. Worse yet, I selected the steepest road because the map only showed it as shorter. Looking always to avoid traffic, I chose unwisely well this time. Only one vehicle had passed this way before me. Only its tracks kept me company on my climb. I can't recall ever making a longer uphill climb on a road—certainly not in a blizzard. Just as the tracks disappeared completely under blowing snow, one car returned miraculously down that winding, drifting slope.

Hard to say who surprised whom more. Given fresh tire tracks to follow, a pedestrian definitely benefitted most. Then these tracks disappeared as well, not due to drifting, but to wind sweeping clear the road, as the peak approached. Once over the top I found the official route where snowplows ran. Downhill I ran, in what seemed the wrong direction, but I could or would take no other. About 20 km uphill in a blizzard generally suffices for me. Any shelter would have suited too, but fortune found the perfect place: The Din Inn (Meligno).

Like the abominable snowman I blew through the door. All my clothes, plus pack, hat, hair and beard, bore a coating of ice and snow. In fact that supplied my only coat. I never hike with any other. After bursting in, I backed out sheepishly to shave off the worst of my frozen fleece. A tureen of soup, meant to feed four, finished thawing me from inside. Or perhaps the warm welcome of my charming hostess worked the charm. She wouldn't have had opportunity to save my life, however, had I not first encountered El Bar del Lago in the vale below and a roadside pilgrim chapel, considerately open, also dedicated to San Rocco. I lit two votive candles: one for my ancient mom, one for reaching a computer to post my survival for her. More utilitarian, I used the flames to dry cold, wet gloves. Fearing snowed-in more than in snow, a toasty traveler emerged from the chapel, and again from the Din Inn above.

The correct direction reconfirmed, I happily headed downhill—rapidly. The startling view opening below would have shocked you too. The sunny Italian Riviera appeared both close and warm. As I bounded down the mountain, I could see where Mother Nature drew a straight line through creation at 1,000 feet of elevation. A green Eden, albeit corrupted, waited under a whited wasteland. Palm trees never looked better.

A word of warning: the way down provides more switchbacks than a cat's tail, yet the long road remains very steep, hurtful to the legs and feet of the overeager backpacker. From first sighting, the shining sea remains a shimmering mirage for hours. That time seems longer if you've overeaten above, because you felt it expected, and did not know when you might eat again. Also, the food tastes very good. Now you are forewarned.

"Finale Marina" sounded an appropriate destination, but I veered west towards a more distant Pietra Ligure as that'll save kilometers tomorrow. That meant also reaching the nausea stage of exhaustion today, before I could find food and shelter at feasible prices. Having beaten the blizzard and surmounted the mountains, I won the final battle too, though I think my guts may be killing me, in more ways than one. For now I'm winning though, without losing too much, and have learned much without too much foolishness—but no one has tallied the totals yet.

Tues. 1/3/11

Any who reckon a stroll along the coast to be the easy choice never tried to walk long distances there. Sometimes you glide along just fine by beachfront property or penetrate picturesque villages like Loano, where selecting your route through a maze of arch-covered alleyways can prove puzzling but not impossible. "Loano" sounds ungenerous, but offers much for free, even to a jaded pedestrian like me. However, just when you're happy with your progress, you arrive at an unbreachable obstacle. Public roads can turn into private ones, gated and guarded. "Attenti Al Cane" could claim the title of most common phrase in Italian. At least Italians carefully fence their animals.

Occasionally, signs do warn of dead ends—but falsely for foot traffic. Sometimes sheer cliff meets sea edge or the river that cut the cliff 10,000 years ago. Naturally, in all that time no one thought to bridge the river where people approach it naturally. As the nearest span (a walled-in railroad bridge) will be forbidden, you'll need to backtrack to find the nearest bridge over the tracks, before guessing again at the best route over the water. Most likely that road will be the one least amenable to pedestrians. Other than the automatically banned autobahn, the one road that strings together these perfect coastal pearls (the A10) runs choked in traffic, on the far side of the tracks from the sea. If your feet find the A10, they'll find they're not wanted there. Cutting in and out along the sea cliffs, occasionally through them, the highway scarcely allows two trucks to pass abreast.

In fact, let me take back anything derogatory ever uttered about Irish roads (though not about Irish drivers). Those blasted byways Providence provided to train me for surviving Italian roads. Let me introduce you to one charmingly quaint Italian folk custom. Before flying around a blind bend on the wrong side of what should be called a one-lane road, drivers give a cheerful beep, beep, beep, beep, translated to: "You gonna die." Though they transmit that message at the last moment possible, I've yet to see anybody die, including me, or even a fender bender. Luckily, however, my hair had turned white long before I faced the harebrains on hairpins. White hair stands out too, especially when standing on end. To give credit, Italian drivers show more consideration of folk on foot than do Irish counterparts. Many heart-stopping races have I run in Erin too, under heavy pack, against heavy trucks, to reach any spot marginally safer than a marginless stretch on which Death tried to catch me. By rights pedestrians should be forbidden, but are not. Indeed, regular bus services ply this route, stopping mid-traffic for anyone waving. Pity a poor pilgrim not permitted public transport, however desperate his plight.

- - - - -

At last Alassio I reached, but alas was misled by promising passageway that beckoned with lying signs. Beguiled into a dark and arcane chicane, I arrived at trespass and trials. In a crumbling estate of terraced olive groves on a hill in the center of town, I stumbled about in the dark. After a fairly mad scramble, I return to possibly public land where I intend to camp, as apparently God means me to do so.

- - - - -

Near midnight, mad baying hounds me from sleep. Surprised earlier by not being surprised by dogs, I'd grown too confident in my escape and may yet face a nasty surprise. Though the baying for blood by a pack does approach, nothing can I do but wait and wonder. Perhaps a security firm that patrols the estate below had alarms triggered and now hunts the culprit. In my favor, no one could have left a wilder trail for the hounds of hell than did I in my back-tracking scramble and confused clambering. Perhaps local gangs of vandals jealously guard their turf, more outraged than the proper owner. Right now, I just hope all the howling won't keep me awake until attacked. I fear more the diabolical cold that dogs my bones and denies rest than I do the devil's dogs outside my tent.

I do confess, as I grow old, so too does the notion that I can do whatever I say I can. I thank today's trials for proving the necessity of yesterday's. Oh, don't forget that all my suffering is offered up for the intentions of all who contribute to our family charities. As plenty of pain will be around, enough to go around, my offer is a bargain. Already my dawgs feel beaten to death. They look and smell like bruised, bloated, blistered, bleeding corpses. May God have mercy on my soles. My left ankle twinges; my left hip displays a seeping packsore. Some pain in the hip might originate internally, making it more worrisome. My pack, lopsided and heavy, seems to press there unduly.

Though not the worst, the ankle worries most. Before I sleep, I shall pray over that. I only know one prayer for healing; I hope it works, appeals to the Almighty as before. Whatever your belief, believe I prayed earnestly yesterday my "pilgrim rosary." This power-prayer may even suit Protestants willing to be pleased. Hey, did I or did I not escape blizzard-bedecked and bedeviled mountains? I am already reassured by the conviction that the worst hike of this Camino now stands completed at the outset and has granted me my hiking legs for the remainder.

Wed. 2/3/11

Other than escaping my tent, and deconstructing it, all seems to have gone well today. The twisted path of last night unwound in daylight and led to the middle way sought. As confidence patted me on the back , it shoved me into hedgerows and olive groves, terraced and impenetrable (all private property). If distance done today on mysterious deerpaths had been hiked in America, I'd have Lyme disease for sure. I hope I haven't got it now, nor any other reaction to noxious weeds and thorns wrestled today.

With an archangel and a big stick, I did fight through to a proper hiking path over peaks not buried under snow. However, this way was very rough, and not very long. Bless whoever laid it though, for bringing me sans snarling traffic to gracious Cervo, a city with the finest beach so far, and much more. Unfortunately, though not her fault, Cervo also provided the first personal threat perceived since Dublin.

The beach could only have been improved by a bikinied body or two. However, at this hour in this season only the beach lies bare. People prefer to display fashion-able winter apparel, however unnecessary. Happy not to be distracted during pilgrimage, I did not object to folks overdoing the covering up, until youths in ski-masks started following me into a dark and deserted part of town. Then I quickly entered the nearest, brightest, ritziest hotel visible, to make pointless inquiries until pursuit passed. Having thanked the considerate receptionist, I continued into what you could only call a mugger's paradise, at least at night. With little lighting, and no escape between cliffs and sea, a public promenade stretches some kilometers to the next town, Imperia, the destination decided for the day. My shoe-heels took some wear, clicking hard through those klicks.

Legs held back for real need, brain and gut ran ahead with a message for muggers: "If you wait for me, you better carry a gun, of large caliber, for I carry hickory. Even if shot in the heart with a peashooter, I will still scatter a pea-brain. Come big or stay home. To take my money, end my quest, you'll need to finish me. With my acid reflux, I can spit in your eye and blind you. Don't diss dyspeptics."

At the end of the promenade, having assured myself that no one waited or followed, I set up home among the shacks of a boat-for-hire business (closed for the season). A bench on the beach, sheltered by an awning and shielded by a table, more than sufficed for my needs. No need to put up (and take down) a tent. Though signs forbid sleeping on the beach, few enforcers could see me before dawn and fewer expect to (in this season). My ankle has healed, incidentally. I'll sleep better for that. No pain worries now, and no doubt about someone watching over me. Good night.

Thurs. 3/3/11

Imperia matches up to its grand title and to Genoa, if not historically, then in antique atmosphere and current commerce and growth. On the cathedral square (Piazza Duomo), I found The Black Horse Bar. If disappointed by staff not speaking English, I enjoyed my usual pantomime, which successfully produced two prisotta ham slices wrapped around an orange segment coated in cream cheese, beside slices of bread and apple cake. Once I'd polished that off, I treated servers to a less polished performance of an Irish folk song in honor of all the Irish stout, beer and spirits served to others or decorating walls.

The cathedral churched me nicely next. That would have sufficed to make me recall Imperia fondly. By happy chance and serious endeavor, I also discover a properly marked Camino trail, the elusive middle way. Having noted indicators before, I finally spy official shell tiles. Hallelujah!

True, shortly I would lose the barely marked trail, but the way I went held a mile-long way of the cross, which for my sins brought me back to Imperia. Ordinarily this would have upset me, but this roundabout route revealed another important part of town. More importantly, my mischance put me providentially on the right road to San Lorenzo—making me "as happy as Larry." At the point of engaging in another suicidal sprint along shoulderless highway, I darted across traffic precisely in time to spot a rough foot-warn path to another quieter road below. This God-send turned up the very start of a rail to trail conversion, of which no tourist info officer had deigned to speak. This perfect present from St. Larry or St. Jim stretches past San Remo. Hallelujah again!

Prior to that, you pass St. Stefano, which would have pleasantly provided my choice for sleeping rough had I not spotted "White Power" graffiti (in English and Italian). Though I look as white as any white could, such signs unsettle me. In the next village, Riva, I locate an ancient church on a very crooked lane. The edifice includes a peculiar feature common on Italian churches. A prominent porch for passing pilgrims (possibly lepers) welcomes me and offers a window for viewing the candlelit interior. The porch provides safe enough shelter in my judgment, and electric light graces it.

I shall sleep the sleep of the justified tonight, as my missteps around Imperia put in my path a professional beggar, the Romany sort, a type typically avoided. However, after availing of the wonders of the world, presented in a western supermarket, and finding the wandering mendicant still silently waiting, I put folding money among the coppers in his cup. On this circulating note I wrote "Pray for the Kingston Familia" because some of them once treated this traveler kindly. The gypsy seemed as genuinely grateful as he did crippled. By gesture he indicated the money would buy food. If that "food" be found in a bottle, I would not begrudge it to this poor fellow.

I post this note now to my readers, not to boast but to confess my action wasn't exceptional except for me. Living as simply as I do, I seldom feel possessed of anything superfluous-to-need. Besides, does not the Bible demand prudent stewardship also? Yet, wasteful largesse some regard as sound investment in heavenly real estate. If I'm quite happy in a tent here (or pilgrim porch), do I need a mansion where the sun always shines?

Fri. 4/3/11

Riva received me as graciously as any village should. To the whole world I recommend The Metropolitan Tea Shop on Via Nino Bixio, offering teas from all the world without losing the village feel. This homeless soul "needed to go" to this shop, but he recommends it even if you don't. The bakery down the street exudes efficiency and good taste, while retaining friendliness. The supermercato farther down had already provided excellent prices and service, when an "unusual" customer acknowledged my pilgrim badge by bestowing on me two pounds of bananas. While I could use pounds of potassium-rich fruit on this pilgrimage, I wouldn't dream of killing myself by eating more than two today or carrying more than two for tomorrow, even if they wouldn't get "killed."

Finding all protest futile, I march away fully laden before my benefactor can give me a big can of sardines.

- - - - -

Then began an unexpectedly difficult task: giving away one pound of bananas. Where's a beggar when you need one? Everybody on the Italian Riviera looks fit and comfortable. Many visit second homes or expensive hotels. Surely someone must know a local charity even if unable to eat a banana themselves. Nope. Nobody. Finally, I convinced a workman to take them. Though he likely only left them in refuse he collected, I never did that.

From Riva this pilgrim progressed promptly to San Remo, to finish the week required to reach the farthest point into Italy ever intended as a starting point. Despite the week, a footsore pellegrino pressed on to his planned goal for day one of pilgrimage: the border city Ventomiglia. Proudly he marched into the night, even if pride is a sin.

Rather than the hiker, let me honor the baker who saved the hiker, and the honor of Italy, by being the first Italian shopkeeper, at the last opportunity possible, to give food for free, in honor of San Giacomo. God bless him.

About San Remo we'll only opine it surely fancies itself equal to Genoa and Imperia. In the 1800s before Italian unification, the city revolted against the Republic of Genoa, albeit unsuccessfully. Local opinion of Imperia expressed in graffiti even I understand: "Imperia = diarrhea." I accuse soccer of producing this venom.

Russian and English nobles surely have been selecting San Remo for centuries, as Orthodox and Anglican churches show. The knowledge and expertise in English (with Irish accent) of a tourist info officer impressed me. She had the essential info on the pilgrimage route just completed! The specially pedestrianized route, including a mile-long tunnel (claustrophobe beware) ends with San Remo, but no walker need fear the road after that town. I did rightly fear finding nowhere to spend the night on the far side of a border town like Ventomiglia. Nowhere afforded both savings and safety. Fixing on the former, I plunked down on very public private property and prayed no one pass that way for a few hours, particularly no policeman. I'm leaving Italy under budget, having only used one hotel in one week here. Pilgrimage suggests uncomfortable travel.

Sat. 5/3/11

Today I prayed three Aves to pass the border police. I didn't suppose I should face difficulty over my passport problem, but no vagabond can ever relax with officialdom, especially at a border. This internal E.U. border still means something to someone, as a traffic tailback demonstrated.

Herds of RVs stood corralled for inspection. Your happy hiker glided by without one word from anyone. From pent-up anxiety a soul sprang over sunbeams into Menton, "the pearl of France." Merci, mon Dieu. I'd have hated to have my entire quest complicated so soon.

A parade greeted my arrival with floats, bands, fancy-dress, and dancers in feathers. Party! Possibly, that's all only part of the annual Lemon Festival, which celebrates Menton's possessing the climate to grow lemons and to drink lemonade. This micro-climate, falsely claimed by the entire Mediterranean region, makes Menton the Rostrevor of France. Totally surrounded by basalt cliffs, except south or seaward, the town captures every sunbeam to avoid winter entirely. Visit for a year; you'll need your camera every day, but never a coat. Victorian Brits, well-informed about it, invalided here to heal consumption, etc.—if they had dosh. I take advantage of the long history of English-speaking visitors, without enjoying their imperial vestiges.

I'm too tired and crabby. Getting to the hostel and early bed proves harder than expected. I'm in no mood to enjoy the festival (too pricey) because I need to put my own show back on the road. Resupply and rest aside, I must clean and sew my wardrobe, and my pack! Its stitching took more damage than imagined. My rig does not appear up to another continent of hard hiking. Perhaps this damage explains some of the injury to a body that requires cleaning and stitching. For now dabs of Neosporin must do, as the hostel looks located on a high hill above the city.

- - - - -

Before quitting Italy and week one of hiking, I acquired injury #7—not counting chapped hands, heartburn, burst heart, burst ear, burst rear, and burst lungs. (Seemingly my breathing is through a sack of shredded spuds.) Mostly attributable to previous conditions, assorted pains allow one hurt to stand out: a peculiar chafing inside my right leg. This afflicts novelly. I fear thorny weeds recently wrestled have wounded me after all. Worse, maybe some parasite's parasites persecute me. If the deer ticks with Lyme have jumped the pond, they've got me at last. How would I know though? If I did not feel tired, sick and sore already, I really would be unwell.

The bad news: after reaching the auberge des jeunesse on the cliffs above town, I discovered it closed, inexplicably contrary to the tourist office, my guidebook and its own sign. The good news: ditto. For the lady managing the nearby campsite allowed a pelerin de St. Jacques to tent for free, and rain looks most unlikely.

CHAPTER 2
Menton to Arles

Sun. 6/3/11

I galloped again to the sound of the bells and made it in time, this time, if not on time—a distinction R.C.s recognize. From St. Michael's Plateau above town to St. Michael's Piazza above Old Town, I raced to miss only the first reading, incomprehensible to me anyhow. For that I fault my study of French, not the Bible. Yet delivery by priest and chanteuse sounded inspiring. Better still, the cathedral only opens for Mass; non-devout tourists must miss out. St. Michael commands the civic coat of arms, and my patron's popularity runs high all along this coast.

Duty done to Sunday dinner too, I returned to the plateau and personal highpoint: my accomplishing all aforementioned chores, plus decamping and descending. On the walk from town, long shadows dragged down my mood, but I marched determinedly towards the disappearing light. In light of disappearing concern for pedestrians (past Menton), that's not easy. You've not seen Monte Carlo till you view its lumination from atop concrete barriers guarding famous cliff-edge roads high above the city. Can't really recommend this dicey view for long. Though not equal to tightrope walking, to fall either way can still mean sudden death, and yet it's safer than hiking in the narrow winding road. Reaching Tarbe at all, and before all restaurants closed, pleased immensely. By that late hour, finding any cheap accommodation seemed a bad bet, and, as most traffic had deserted the roads, I pressed on downhill.

Misdirection put me on the route that mysteriously ended the life of Princess Grace. Oddly, I too veered from the corniche and nearly killed myself, though not in a sports car. Accidentally discovering a marked trail that promised a shortcut to Villefranche-sur-Mer, I took it to Whacky World. Probably a project that popped with the housing bubble, an aborted development ended in a twelve-foot fence above the road required. What choice had I?

The fence did not present an impossible obstacle. The rock climb would look entertaining if you're not the fool doing it with pack, pouches, and staff. Smacking myself in the eye with a pine branch could only have been topped by falling backwards into the road, under a truck. Sorry to disappoint, slapstick fans, no truck. When I did slip, serious injury from landing with extra weight could've ended my camino then and there, but I limped on until a wall of weariness stopped me cold, after midnight. A concrete slab, roofing a derelict cliff-dwelling below the road, may not sound inviting. Try looking at it after walking there all night from Menton, nearly to Eze.

Mon. 7/3/11

Nice to see Nice; not so nice getting here. The way was eased by Eze where two kilos of goods I mailed after judging unnecessary my carrying those items over the complete Camino. The pretty postmistress has put quite a spring in my step by accepting the weight. Soured by all my questions in questionable French, she grew sweeter at the end and bestowed sweets on a pelerin de St. Jacques. Yeah, more than I care to carry or to eat. Though she finally understood me, she still seems to have missed my point. Worse, she has given me a new deadline. The post office allows only three weeks to catch up with my package in St. Jean Pied de Port on the far side of France.

In lighter mood regardless, I should have better appreciated the promenade magnifique into Nice. It wound a touch too much for wounded feet and winded frame, however, and Villefranche failed to match my memory of it—probably not the fault of Villefranche. Guess I ought not to have gone out of my way for her (for either this antique city on the sea, or the her I once brought here).

I reckoned stopping in Nice for Mardi Gras to be OK, not out of the way, but alas, I was mistaken again. Due to dubious weather, or more doubtful criterion, civic authorities declared Thursday Fat. We'll call that a sign from God for due diligence before Ash Wednesday. A proper pilgrim penance seems appropriate to Lent, though not purposely made. Just don't ask me to give up sweets as well!

As Nice provided my original airport choice, I decided to try sleeping there tonight, on my way out of town, but discovered that nice idea was not a good idea, as the terminals all shut down at midnight, and not very nicely. That renders better my choice of Milan though. Another difference between airports, Milan offers one chapel to all, all night: a Catholic one. Nice, a near neighbor, provides a non-denominational Christian chapel, a mosque, and a Jewish temple (all closed). America would generally go with one meditation room. In the end, I had not a prayer of staying in that airport. Still, it served my needs better than I had right to expect. I'll hang around a bit longer tomorrow to use the facilities. As the route should run flat, we'll see where walking flat out leaves me.

Mardi Gras, Tues. 8/3/11

Find Nice pretty? Looks pretty ugly to me. Try walking out of France's 5th largest city. See if you don't see her as fat and sprawling. Odd to think that Nice, all Provence, didn't even belong to France until 1860. Looks like the choice came down between Napoleon III or Garibaldi. Nice tends towards reactionary. Likewise, my safe byway became highway, excluding poor pedestrians. Only trespass prevented backtracking. I could have stopped to enjoy small villages, strategically and photogenically set above small coves en route to Cannes. I could even claim I did stop—but I did not. The title "beautiful" could apply to today's march only if success impresses: a forced march, Nice to Cannes, in time for Mardi Gras. No plunder did I win though. What's French for Thin Tuesday?

My sole celebration consisted of employing a toilet in a five-star hotel, which, even so, offered no hot water. For a coeliac sufferer, the French for "bread" (*pain*) grows ever more appropriate. Nevertheless, the concierge's granting me use of the ritzy facility in honor of St. Jacques I did appreciate. Outside, I got to listen to a busker play genuine classic French accordion music. Explaining that his notes came to me as a blessing from God, I offered my appreciation in paper (unusual to buskers) with a message inscribed: "For my sister Katie. Play and pray for her." I knew my sister would want this old man to continue playing the old music on the promenade of Cannes.

Detained by no other celebration, I feel Provence and Providence push me onward. Or maybe Satan presses me past my endurance. Casting about for a place to lay low, my staggered body received a push from two yahoos fire-bombing a car in the street beside me. Sacre Bleu!

Made quite the flash and bang. That might also describe my disappearance. This Belfast boy would caution the two delinquents not to stand so close when lighting up a car. They did rapidly put distance between them and the scene of the crime by ripping away on a motorbike, leaving a foreign vagabond to take the blame. I wouldn't even retain my usual ability to blather my way away from trouble.

I have no time to spare for dancing with gendarmes. A couple klicks on, I have located a supermarket trolley shed that suits me well enough. I have at least managed to walk off another map (another scrap of paper to discard).

Ash Wednesday 9/3/11

Yes, when out "searching for yourself," you sometimes find out what you do not want to know. *Toujours le toilette est problematique.* Pardon my French. Underway, I resolve again, against caution, to seek a middle way as it looks shorter and quicker if I just keep up speed uphill. I had intended going around by the sea through San Raphael, for nostalgia's sake, but since I only tripped when last tripping down memory lane, I've changed my mind.

As Lenten penance, for the sins of disappointing and dis-appointment, I have taken the high and hard road, literally and figuratively, forgiving transgressors as I would have them forgive me. I also like the notion of all week walking on one route (lucky #7). No more experimenting (getting lost). The coast would cost more dawdling too. Having coasted for a week, I change course. In San Raphael's favor, I recall it offering the best beach on this coast.

- - - - -

The elusive middle way again fails to emerge, as I stumble over the 1,000 ft. marker again. However, we're a week away from the Italian Alps' weather. The way proves pleasant enough, though clouds showed a foreboding tinge this a.m. I'm proud to have braved the mountain way anyway. The even more elusive diminutive "native" deer I spotted here. Marring the peace of this ravine, a marker memorializes a resistance fighter assassinated by the Gestapo up here. Strange to imagine the world at war in this quiet ravine in a united Europe. Comrades of this victim may yet live. Hell, they probably still pedal up to fire a salute.

Not much farther, I stop to shoot a photo reminiscent of the Appalachian Trail. Tourists don't usually associate France with forested ridges as far as the eye can spy. The biggest difference? Cork trees form most of the forest here, and have been harvested too (stripped of bark to about eight feet up the trunk). These smallish trees of the scrub oak family show leaves and limbs that suggest holly.

Another strange growth flourishes up here. Up the back road to San Raphael, a bum stumbles upon some of the most exclusive gated communities on the planet. "Domaines" own everything but the public highway, and jealously eye that. When attractive footpaths or quiet streets may provide private police patrols or guarded gates at the far end, exploring "shortcuts" loses a lot of the usual appeal for me. A beckoning laneway may curve as seductively as she pleases; I'll not get shot for a pretty path.

Funny, ain't it, how fortified towns on remote outcrops have returned to fashion? Of course, they contribute to the societal collapse their rich denizens attempt to flee. Wait till expensive cars can no longer bring fat asses to cliff tops.

Then all will need to meet their pseudo neighbors, none of whom have ever needed to share before, or used hands and heads for anything more useful than making cocktails.

Way up here among the high and mighty, St. James has placed a pace-setter to push me over high mountains. If heaven sent, he looks no angel, more spoiled scion. Typical teen, he slouches along, earphones blocking out the world he cannot control with contempt. At least his pants don't ride his knees as they would in America. Frenchie lurches right along. Young or old, Europeans look far fitter than Yanks. This young man presses me. He'd impress, did he not stride down the middle of the wrong lane, nearly getting me hit by a car. He must just feel too precious to die mundanely. Abruptly he does disappear, as if clipped by a car or magically removed by St. Jim. He may have been the pillion passenger on a motorbike that passed. He deserves credit for helping me reach Frejus within minutes of a self-imposed deadline, despite my stopping to collect jewelry off the road. Curves cause centrifugal force to leave pendants on asphalt, and possibly more precious cargo. The curves put me around the bend, again insane, running on concrete barriers off cliff-cutting roads. How's that for fit? Not bad for an old man, but not good for him.

Folks seem pretty fit economically too, in Northern Italy and Southern France. Due to TV, I fully expected to view more distress. Beggars do abound, but look like the incorrigible, professional sort. I don't note many businesses going belly up. Something, in the state socialism of the tradition-bound French, conserves companies from failure. Even less will state-capitalists in "Communist" China permit failure. Only America, and other Third World nations, hail failure as victory for economic Darwinism, though many of its proponents propound against evolution. I would object less to the inherent waste (of money, effort and resources) if the fittest truly did survive, but in our crony capitalism the most corrupt win. Corruption never indicated health or vitality.

I commend "community-capitalism." Under this ism capitalists would approach a community for permission to exploit it. The county board (community re-presenters, not "representatives") would explain what any capitalist would need to invest contractually in that community (in terms of jobs, benefits, services, discounts, etc.) in return for a guarantee against cut-throat, cut-rate competition. For, in America the race does not go to the fast and fit, but to the fast buck and the morally unfit. They leave their victims lying like corpses on our community's streets. Why do we tolerate this terrible waste of the world's resources? This sin will shortly end the world as we know it.

10/3/11 Thurs.

Good news/bad news. Last night I rolled over in my sleeping bag onto my packsore. Yet, no profane yelp of pain escaped my lips to spoil sacred pilgrimage or to alert anyone to my innocuous trespass. Combining a rolled sweatshirt on the hip, with Neosporin in the wound, works wonders. Salve saves my inner thigh as well. Bad news goes to all who count on my offered up pain to escape purgatory. You may need plan B. Moreover, all who depend on my packsore to prevent my completing my Camino, and their paying up on pledges, may also feel disappointed.

More good news and bad. Bad for me, I probably won't reach Santiago in time. Boldly adding a week in Italy proves foolhardy, if practical. Airfare to Milan came cheaper than to

Nice, but I ought not to have begun walking so soon. Here to hike, I trust God and St. James. Good news for sponsors, they probably won't have to pay up after all. However, I do have a plan B: Just reaching Navarette in Spain will still double the distance of my previous pilgrimage and return me to the golden scene of my mini-miracle and sacred pledge. Don't let that worry your wallets though. Remaining determined to push all the way to Santiago, I'll most likely never reach Navarette.

If I hike into Arles on Monday morning, I'll be back on schedule, though in what condition to continue, or in what condition the Camino continues, God only knows. Already suffering serious illness, this pilgrim hasn't slept well for a week and fears the flu on top of previous infections. Of course this coeliac also poisons himself daily, and each of his knees have popped for no known reason. Don't forget this very pen and page delays your diarist. Readers, you hold me back. Have you no pity?

On the bright side, weather stays on the bright side. Sure, I beat a blizzard at the outset, but that only blew me onto the right course. I'm fine ever since. Don't misunderstand, the weather has not been fine; I have been fine with the weather. Doesn't do to complain about climate. Honestly, no hiker would prefer warmer weather, except perhaps at night. I'm daily surprised in the a.m. to find no frost. Mercury must hit hard at forty at least. My number one advice (after not carrying this much cash when sleeping rough): invest in your sleeping bag. Just what more I can demand from my chronically ill, old body, I do not know. I do know that tripling my pilgrimage, by walking upright into Santiago, would constitute another miracle for Jesus and St. James. In fact, I bet I don't make it, pledging cash for pilgrims if I do.

I enjoy myself with the French language and cheese anyway, two matters the French take too serious. I win the cheese game as long as I find cheeses unknown to me but edible by me. All choices so far please my palate. Usually you have to lie a little to say that in France. Mendacity wouldn't do for a mendicant pilgrim of St. Jim. Hey, anyone ever find a better dessert apple to devour with cheese than a Pink Lady from New Zealand? (Not from France!)

The language game goes like this: I ask in French; the French reply in English. Or, they reply in French, and I pretend to comprehend, nodding sagely, like a fool. The game grows even more fun when I really do understand. Pointing almost always works, and isn't cheating. Loving the tone and meter of French, I enjoy most its verbosity. On the front of a full, off-duty, or out-of-service bus, the French sign reads "This autobus, it is not taking on travelers." On internationally recognized yellow triangular signs, "yield" is superfluous; the French write, "*Cedez le passage.*" French requires two words to say "Not." 'Nuff said.

Seriously on language: hiking across Europe has made me appreciate how much we lose by failing to maintain our monolingual culture in America. One language covering a continent gave a huge economic advantage, but also a social one. The inability even to communicate a disarming phrase or pleasant greeting renders a society less social. "*Bonjour*" or "*Hola*" does not suffice. Just being civil grows problematic here. In defense of France I add that an inability to communicate makes more amazing a big bottle of water just gifted to this foreign pilgrim.

- - - - -

The same pilgrim may have been given water again that night, in a manner much less special or pleasant. Prior to that incident I had trudged in darkness from Vidauban to LeCamet. Looking about for where to lay my head, I felt a little alarmed when a stranger pulled up his car beside me, to gun his engines angrily before squealing off to the dark end of the street, where he halted his car and shut off the lights. Feeling uncertain about trying to walk past, I stalled a bit. The car barked back to life and did a U-turn to brake hard opposite to where I'd walked. At this point I feared the driver feared my trespassing on his property.

I had already noted that prostitution and racketeering operate openly along the highways of France. Attempting to watch from the shadows, I observed the driver repeat the process, before abandoning his car to walk past the tree I hid behind. Presumably his vehicle has broken down somehow, but I gave him a good head start and crossed the road to hike. Hoping he didn't lurk up ahead, I kept a sharp eye and a blunt instrument ready for him.

Another klick brought me to where I wanted to wake when businesses open. As the starry night suggested needing no shelter, I picked a dry stretch of concrete, a little out of the way, to build my nest, but recognized the need to vacate before dawn. This, my weary body failed to do. Waking, I was not entirely surprised to discover suspiciously heavy dew on my sleeping bag. This dew did not smell suspicious, thank God, and I'd heard no zipper or snicker during the night. Zippo fluid my nose would also detect, even without a lighter. A 500 ml bottle of water could supply this much damp, damned entertainment for a wicked waster. I resolve not to move on until I find a laundry anyway.

I really can't recommend how I travel. This near the ground, travel grows too dirty and dangerous to be fun. If able to afford more time, never mind money, I would. Now I must waste a morning rounding up a toilet, laundry and supermarket. Miraculously, St. Jim wrangled all three for me in the immediate vicinity—plus a choice even.

Laundromats grow quite scarce in France and really take you to the cleaners. The same might be said of public/private lavatories. Supermarkets pop up everywhere now though. I remember, as an American, regretting their absence once. The destructive nature of the hypermarket should be decried here, but this ravenous consumer cannot bring himself to do it. On an aside, public phones still decorate every corner, though no one uses them anymore.

Fri. 11/3/11

On the road again, near noon, I swear to put in a full day's hike yet. Won't leave much time for writing.

- - - - -

From LeCannet to Tourve you can't call a bad day's work. The countryside remains the same. Provence famously produces olives, lavender, sunflowers and more, but nothing shows now save dormant vineyards. I woke up one vineyard, one claiming a connection to Templars (presumably a recent exploitation of resumed notoriety). With a hickory stick I rattled a roadside lance and shield. The rogues will think twice about challenging me twice.

What the hiker finds discarded along the highway can provide distraction. Was it yesterday that three pieces of jewelry appeared in a tight pattern? Today, three books (in French) lay crumpled, about a kilometer apart. Maybe a motorist had time to judge a book by its back cover before chucking each out the window. Perhaps a pilgrim like myself judged each in turn too heavy to carry farther. As an author I object to this disregard for literature and littering; as a backpacker, I understand. I can't take it too personal, as one of those books is a Bible.

Tourve attained provided real excitement. Exhausted, I seek only sleep but meet late at night in the entrance of this village a local motorcycle gang. Great! No Hell's Angels, these yahoo youth yearn to show grown-ups, by acting child-ishly, how grown up the children have become. No, I don't understand either. Apparently, balancing on anything with two wheels and loud engines proves maturity if you travel at unsafe speeds, especially on only one wheel. As these leaky vessels of untested testosterone on beat-up motorbikes appear the very sort to beat up an old hobo (a foreigner to boot), a game of cat and mouse ensues, though the cat may not know it...

I managed to traverse the town, hide my pack, locate a "latrine" and "camping ground," all without being seen. Before erecting my tent, I needed only to retrieve my pack. At the worst moment possible, naturally, the bikers roared up, to spot me entering the local footie grounds. How better could I excite their territorial instinct?

Turning to run at that point would only spur the chase instinct. As the yobs already looked occupied in adrenaline high jinks, I just moved out of sight, maybe out of mind, into a hastily picked place only open to frontal attack. Putting my pack behind me, holding my stick before me, I waited...

Counting on the short attention spans of today's youth, I put my exhaustion on pause for an eternity (about twenty minutes) while the boyos played. When they suddenly departed, I considered leaving, but thought they might wait and watch as well. Too tired to do more, I picked the darkest corner of the practice pitch to pitch my tent.

Sat. 12/3/11

Quelle surprise! I'm alive. I'd meant to stay awake for another hour (till 1:00 a.m.), to see if the hunt pack returned, but I dropped into dreamland before I even climbed into my sleeping bag. Now that should mean I was indeed "out cold," but miraculously my drafty tent stayed warm last night. In morning light I find the town hugged by chapel-topped cliffs and do feel supernaturally embraced. In this light (and light mood) any town might appeal, but I do declare that Tourve charms me. To be alive here feels so good, I would live here for good if Life allowed.

Of course, all the yahoos still lie in bed now. To be fair to towns passed yesterday, LeCannet and Flasson also retain their ancient character while maintaining a vibrant village life. Many of the most celebrated, cultivated medieval villages merely present a pretentious façade for tourists, for the benefit of blow-in artists and artisans. In Flasson though, I could imagine veterans of the *résistance* sitting in the square named for them, discussing exploits. In Tourve the quality of village life appears transparently clear. Water channeled constantly along the streets, a medieval or Roman sewer system, renders the entire town into a fountain. Authorities should post non-potable signs.

- - - - -

Just passed by fifty motorcycle cops on no apparent mission. Like a parade of chausseurs, mounted and helmeted, they swept past in pairs, all glistening in the sun. I felt compelled to salute, and they, appreciating appreciation, nodded and smiled. That's good, as I've seen these fine fellows at work when they weren't smiling.

The next town geographically also comes next in order of appeal in this procession of towns. The mini-city of St. Maximum offers a 13th century basilica with the remaining remains of a 1st century saint: none other than Mary Magdalene. OK, maybe it doesn't, but the history of the place remains fascinating, and well presented. Of all the ecclesiastical buildings ever visited, I put this one in the top ten for enlightening experience. I seem to collect pilgrimage churches like beads on a rosary. The legend of Mary Magdalene offers special significance, figuring in the topical gnostic heresy and Albigensian Crusade, crucial in this region I traverse physically and philosophically. I am gnostic, like the local Cathars, but not heretically. I probably dally longer than probity commends, as I face a 50 km hike to Aix de Provence. Let's hope that city continues the progression in appeal.

- - - - -

Nope, all I have to show for 50 km are Aix and pains. Can't really blame Aix for being a modern, prosperous, metropolis, but first contact—a harsh response to a request for directions—doesn't auger well. I hoped two Irish pubs might provide more hospitality. Less. The Irishness of said establishments ends with the signs outside. No owner, management, or staff could lay any claim to Ireland.

Prices in inns and hotels climb in Aix too and don't include breakfast. The hospitality shortage is explained by the thousands of college students present, keeping demand high, and expectation low. No one complains overly, as more than one famous university draws here the most attractive female populace (dressed to party) I have ever encountered anywhere. Three cute co-eds tried to help one poor ancient traveler find a bed. No, the welcome ended there.

This is Saturday night too, "Samedi Gras" even. (Isn't France's abandoning Mardi Gras embarrassing?)

- - - - -

In only one respect does Aix not disappoint. On arrival I stumbled upon Le St. Jean de Malte Eglise, the church of the crusading order of St. John, i.e., the Hospitalers, or the Knights of Malta. I must try fittingly to find it tomorrow for Sunday Mass. This 13th century church, built to bury Berengers, Dukes of Provence (and Catalonia), is attached to a priory that once housed pilgrims and now keeps a museum. Much as I love art, I'd have preferred a cheap bed.

To further dampen my evening, rain falls steadily. For more than a fortnight, I have tripped through the spring season without once breaking out my poncho. Thank you, Jesus. I guess You need to hear the prayers of farmers too. Until now, St. James has only employed sharp rowels of rain to spur my pilgrim progress. The wind today (50 m.p.h.) literally pushed me up the road. Thanx again.

Sun. 13/3/11

Sorry, Mom. Last-minute arranging, to avoid hotel surcharges (on an already contested bill) made me late for Mass. Having placed me near the bus station, good sense directed me that way, to implement a plan that might save my feet from another brutal race like yesterday's. Yet, trusting in St. Jean (patron of pilgrim protectors), I turned towards his church, in the hope that its doors had not yet been locked.

Turns out, I'd not missed Mass at all, due to the celebrant's fondness for his own voice (a very good one). In a surprisingly crowded church (in a heathen city), the liturgy was entirely sung, running one and a half hours. In English I might have stood that (and the French do stand through most of Mass), but in French, I doubt it. Thank you, Jesus, for your small mercy of letting me be late. I do know the clouds of incense would've killed one Berenger I know.

Afterwards, the priest picked the pilgrim out of the crowd to present him with a present and a blessing. "From there I flew away, spirits never failing, landing at the quay, just as a *bus* was sailing." St. John has kindly timed everything ideally for me. I'll land in Arles in good time to execute my plan to save my slaughtered feet. After an entire day of hurrying under heavy pack and heavy clouds, along an unknown road to a strange and unpleasant destination yesterday, I reckon today I'll let my head help me out of some hard hiking tomorrow.

En route to Aix, I felt compelled repeatedly to run like a hero into the "gap of death" when two trucks or buses met (with me) on a narrow bridge or walled lane. You'd be impressed to see knees and heels flying, pack and pouches bouncing, stick and hat held high, white mane and whiskers whipping in the wind. Adrenaline fed, my body came pumping 'n' puffing like pistons on a steam engine. Motorists slowed to applaud the performance.

"I'll ache tomorrow," I thought, "like I'd been hit by one of these juggernauts." Later, a score of jabbing pains in my legs reminded me to let up soon, or face the consequences. That's when head said to feet, "Take a bus from Aix (*aches*) to Arles, where hiking was originally to have started two weeks ago.

A readjusted schedule made it my deadline for Monday, but arriving on Sunday could prove wiser to garner Camino info from church authorities. Even cleverer would be locating a place to stay and to store my pack, before returning to Aix and a hard hoe back to Arles. Sunday was set to be wet, not sunny, no day for backpacking anyway. If I made it a day of rest and recovery as God dictates, and then pushed hard all day Monday, with the help of God I could nearly put my poor feet back on a feasible schedule.

- - - - -

Arles shows itself worthy of an extra day. I only regret not staying longer, like another madman did to calm nerves (Van Gogh). The same tree-lined lanes remain to soothe the soul. Cypress, poplar, and plane trees sentry more chaotic roads though. Officials also think wise driving nails into tree trunks, so to hang rubbish bags for collection. Strange fruit. Yet most of Arles remains entirely unchanged, even from Roman times. An amphitheater and coliseum are still employed to entertain the populace. Surprisingly, Spanish bullfighters perform their bloody ballet here, but Provence possesses its own form of non-fatal bullfighting—not to the bull at least. If you can snatch a bag from between a bull's eyes, and escape from the ring alive, you live.

Were Christians ever forced into this contest?

Though unable to find the cheap accommodation sought, I probably could have, and did find an excellent bargain in L'Hotel de L'Amphitheatre. Four-star elegance and customer care belie the two-star cost. Lying here in comfort, watching TV for the first time in three weeks, I find discomfiting my eying the world coming to an end for so many in Japan, and maybe elsewhere. I feel pressed again to hurry on to Santiago and to home.

(P.S.: Before I hit Aix, in the pouring rain Saturday, I experienced the disregard most drivers show pedestrians, but two motorists stopped (unsolicited) to offer lifts (unaccepted). More car horns granted friendly toots than angry honks to a proud and pitiful pilgrim. Odd, *n'est ce pas*, how easily detectable is the difference in horn blasts?)

Mon. 14/3/11

4:00 a.m. is early rising for me, of questionable wisdom health-wise. You ride with me on the 6:15 bus to Aix. one and a half hours will put us there, but each minute of it bothers my battered feet, facing 80 km of hard hiking back. Blistered, bloodied, bandaged again yesterday, my feet need more than ninety minutes to return, and aren't allowed on autobahns. Bound by oath and pilgrim code, they will still carry kilos of extra weight each step to Santiago. A pilgrim must remain self-sufficient. Eighty kilometers, a long way for one day in a foreign land, may render me lost, lame or lazy. If ready for whatever happens today, I still left much weight waiting, stuff not needed for months. Yet, the press of decision weighs heavily on me. For cheapskate pledgers who root for failure, be happy that (for the first time in my life) I carry a spare tire of the odd unlosable fat that indicates lard in the heart and imminent attack.

Tues. 15/3/11

Good thing I came prepared for lost, lame and lazy, because I did not make it back to my pack (sleeping bag or tent), to say nothing of a hotel bed. What I brought had to suffice, but did not work as well as it ought to have. Execution proved more at fault than did design during a pretty miserable night for me. For all my troubles, I did cover about 70 km before my 11 p.m. deadline in Arles turned impossible to hit. Kind strangers insisted I not pay for a ham pizza. I also had to accept water from an opened bottle today, which (though free) broke a rule I had kept while walking the whole way across America. Indicates my desperation. May God preserve me, and all who aid me.

Aha! I've found in my shoe the single grain of sand that produced a blister the size of a silver dollar. One disadvantage of hiking in low shoes is the ease with which one shoe can kick a speck of sand into the other one. Failing to soak my feet in brine, or to rub in oil, I need to try the double-sock trick, despite not packing enough.

- - - - -

With a hotel room to enjoy and utilize to the max, I was determined to take today easy. Eighteen klicks I clicked off quite easily this evening, just to be back where I started. Starting to lag, I invented a pilgrim treat, called a Santiago Sandwich: cold roast pork from a deli, inserted between two apple-tarts. Delightful and filling. Weather never turned so wet that I regret coming out to complete what still leaves me a day late, and more than a dollar short.

Sunday, I met two pilgrims in Arles, (the first so far) who were surrendering to weather and entraining for Spain. They hoped to hike from brighter Barcelona. The first fellow coughed badly, hacking on me over the slight shield of his hand, before offering the same to shake. More than his cold and the cold weather put him off *le chemin*. This experienced pilgrim from Italy found the French cold, and France costly, to pellegrini. He had himself organized a line of pilgrim shelters in parishes across Italy. Don't I wish I'd met him sooner!

Arles disappointed me too, with its high rainfall and low support. Maybe the locals feel pissed off as well by the weather, though reportedly nothing unusual here. I've always experienced and imagined Provence as dry and warm. While struggling alone from Italy, I expected help in Arles. My false illusions at fault, I ought not to blame Arles.

St. Pat's Eve, Wed. 16/3/11

To honor Ireland's patron, I performed atypically today. First, I left a large tip for a chambermaid, Patricia, in the name of another Patrick (more generous than I) and his Kathleen. Of course an incomprehensible note wished a grand day to accompany cash. Then I tried backwards-busking: singing Irish songs while giving away money, etc., to poor pilgrims. I reckoned I can busk because the above Pat isn't singing in the same country, but my efforts disappoint. Two hours earned €5.00, snatched by a young yahoo while I tried to donate. Quite unnecessarily, off he sprinted. He would never understand even if I spoke better French. I'd not much luck giving first aid or food either, until handing it over to professionals, church representatives of Le Chemin de Compostela. (Church and cloister on this square I recommend to other pilgrims even if not in need of my bandages.) In defense of my busking, I must add that the sky let down lashings of rain throughout, and cracked the whip too. Some blamed my caterwauling.

CHAPTER 3
Arles to Toulouse, France

Regardless of my difficulties there, I liked Arles—until I tried to leave. Then I discovered that markers inlaid in the sidewalk didn't kindly guide me out of town—*au contraire.* A torturously twisting route returned me to where I started. To be fair, the way would have seemed pleasant if not done under pack "on a dark and rainy night."

Deciding to discover my own way out, via traffic signs, I found their directions very misleading for a hiker. Finally, forbidden to take on foot the right road, I was shunted into a concrete tunnel in the underbelly of a bridge over the wide River Rhone. Talk about a mugger's alley! Previous tunnels, described as shadowy or dodgy, were never near as dangerous as this entrance to Hades. All hope abandoned, I ran down this slaughter chute into inky darkness, save for the flashing of my mini flashlight. Fearing to find the far end blockaded, I galloped towards the gauntlet of whatever gang lay in wait. When something tripped me, I wasn't even surprised to fall flat and hard. The pain felt lessened by the full expectation of explosive pain from blows bound to fall before I could rise.

Yet, the only crack lay in the sidewalk. The raised lip of that crack sneered to catch my unsuspecting foot. Not crippling me, the accident only made me run faster, until the chunnel shot me out into a darkened public estate.

Let's not call the place derelict, but a derelict car did decorate the sidewalk. Presumably abandoned by joyriders, it wasn't burnt out at least. Unable to continue in the direction desired, an intrepid traveler tried another, and another, before breaking out by a bog path muggers and joyriders made escaping cops. Unhappily, my relief made me happy with the wrong route to Montpelier. Attempts to correct later would put me on the most ridiculously crooked road outside of Ireland. Eventually its turnings did take me to St. Giles, where a shopping-cart shed welcomed me.

St. Paddy's Day, Thurs. 17/3/11

Whatever you've heard about the poor work ethic of French folks, I was impressed, and depressed to find that the market's management and staff showed up before 5:30 a.m. for an 8:30 opening. Managers began by cleaning the parking lot, consigning me to a hard day's work. On ~~two and a half~~ 2½ hours of sleep I'm meant to hup 56 km to Montpelier, after yesterday's long schlep, of which 12 to 20 km ended up superfluous. I'm doing this on a highway that allows one inch for any foot traffic. To stay alive and healthy I have had to trespass through orchards, nurseries and vineyards, about a dozen properties before lunch. That's a rich diet even for me, and ordinarily is not the way to stay alive and well when traveling. Finally I've opted for a long trespass: a track that tracks the train tracks.

I'm down to my last swallow of water, and have nowhere near to buy more. As desperate as my situation stands, I have to feel pretty good about not feeling worse.

- - - - -

Every town in this region seems to have a fixation with bulls. Pamplona in Spain has nothing on Provence. Traffic signs warn of "Manifestations Tourines." Fortunately, I'm just missing all the manic manifestations here, and will traverse Pamplona long before the madness arrives there in July. You can decide for yourself what's wise.

- - - - -

Walking myself into the ground ain't my notion of properly celebrating St. Paddy's Day. I imagined I'd be by now in Montpelier, recalled as lively and lovely, plus cosmopolitan. However, I needed to lie down midday. Though hiking 50 km regardless, I could not defeat the rough edge of the city. Sharply driven back repeatedly against the unbeatable autobahn, I battled on until, bloody and dizzy, I needed to lie down without more ado. Without good maps, I had no recourse other than public scrubland passed by chance. Erecting a tent seemed unnecessary and too tiring anyway. I'm reasonably confident in staying warm and dry tonight. Here's an important trick discovered: use a rolled-up tent as a cushion; create another cushion by stuffing all clothing (in plastic bags) into a sweatshirt; one seat cushion should be carried; supplement the cushions with every newspaper, book and map packed. The pack itself provides the largest cushion. Nobody should need more to sleep comfortably through the night. I won't.

To all who think I've bitten off more than I can chew, I reply, "That's true, but, have you ever seen me eat?"

Fri. 18/3/11

I did make one concession in Arles: not detouring to LePuy as planned. A long-held dream to hike from LePuy deterred already by winter, I'd promised myself a daytrip by bus. However, the info folks look at me like I'm insane when I look for transport to LePuy. I accept their ignorance as a God's wisdom pushing me on. Relentless, isn't He? Another allowance taken in Arles: I finally buy and employ an umbrella.

- - - - -

Walking so much at night, I ascertain why the French eat frogs and snails. If they didn't, they'd be eaten out of house and home. I suggest they eat faster. They may want to start chomping too on lizards that over-run everywhere. Try a fry in butter and basil. *Moi? Non, merci.*

Also slightly unsettling at night, white horses of Le Camargue appear like phantoms along the road. This breed only turns white as adults, staying black or brown until four, a very desirable genetic trait where gypsy horse-traders principally operate, unprincipledly.

In the morning I woke up to less pleasure in my campsite pick. It's crawling with insects, including a tick, making me decamp ASAP. In daylight I sought information from anyone visible, and anywhere open. A McD's I accepted as a godsend. Entering not just to use a toilet and a table, I found the food quite far from U.S. fare. The French faux-version of McDonald's comes closer to the real thing than does the Froggy Mickey Dee's. Not that I'm complaining. I prefer the French version, but how many American kids would be happy with the following Happy Meal: toasted ham and cheese sandwich; ten cherry tomatoes; one carton 100% juice; one bio-yogurt drink?

Further fortified from the supermarket opposite, I relaunched my march in Montpelier successfully. I don't even want to know how many extra kilometers this stranger in town required to reach Le Centreville.

Once in, to find a first-rate *auberge des jeunesse* (youth hostel) delighted, as they accept a pilgrim pass as a membership card (though the latter costs far more). More excitingly, I discovered a fine refuge pour pelerins, i.e., fine if it's not busy. I had the place to myself. Here in Montpelier, I finally receive the sort of reception I'd hoped to find for pilgrims— appropriately in the hometown of St. Roch (Rocca). The refuge hides directly behind St. Roch's Church. Before the church, note an unreal refuge, all the more fun for that. Nearby, on Place de St. Come, even more remarkably, I enjoy a real Irish pub still celebrating St. Pat.

Dia duit, FitzPatrick's, to all who drink and sing there. They let me sing a song and seemed to appreciate it.

Sat. 19/3/11

My right foot looks dreadful. Don't ask how it smells. I've had no opportunity for days to examine it. Good sense dictates taking better care of my feet if I mean for them to carry me to the sea. Relieved to leave the refuge after showering, I could not bring myself to abandon yet the sweet streets around it. The most blasé would be hard-pressed not to be impressed with this delightful enlightened city.

C'est bon, I went nowhere, as I realized, at the last moment, that this sunny day had let me forget my brelly. Unfortunately, no one waits at the refuge, so I must wait. If I carry on, you know the rain will start and never stop for a fortnight. Maybe St. Roch knows I need rest, and my journal requires work. Luckily, I left a more generous donation than usual at the refuge, so I won't be embarrassed to return, except for my dementia. A person back home, who requested prayers for "folks lost, but looking," may look for prayer from there.

My only real regret comes from failing, despite extra time, to join chess players on Le Grand Promenade.

At least while waiting I was entertained by Stef on the steps of St. Roch's. He really knows his clarinet, but not "Danny Boy." *C'est dommage.*

Though successful, had I known how long I would need to wait, I would have left without that umbrella and pyrrhic victory. Your pelerin would have also missed a free pastry from a patisserie however. This blessing offers richness not counted in cash or calories.

Something else I might have missed, however, is ptomaine poisoning. I don't blame the pastry, as I saw my bread handled by the boulanger after he coughed on his hand. Later, a butcher would serve me cooked meat directly after shifting raw cuts, without waiting for water, soap or gloves. Just to further ensure my death, after dinner I dropped the top of my water bottle. In the USA I would not have let any of that pass. *En France, c'est le vie.*

On the bright side, I'm past Montpelier and Grabels on a real *chemin de San Jacques,* and at the first "mile-marker." 1556 km to go. That indicates I've come more than half way in less than half the time. *C'est bon, n'est ce pas?* If only I can believe it, I would die happy with that effort. For now I'll be glad just to find somewhere to sleep…

The place picked appears again to fit under the category of undeveloped public land. I do hope I'm not reclining on a toxic dump or doggy dump. I could wake up with worse than fleas.

Sun. 20/3/11

Waking in the middle of the night, I discovered having drifted off while scribbling before fully cocooning in my sleeping bag. Now that I'm cold, there'll be trouble the rest of the night. Damn.

- - - - -

Rose at 8 a.m. to make Montarnaud before noon. Pleased with the distance, 40 km from Montpelier hostel, I'd have reached here last night but for leaving my brelly, and I would have still made Mass this morning, had Satan not led me astray onto a poorly marked path. The black bastard did it again after Montarnaud, bringing me back to town nearly. As an evil labyrinth of ATV trails (mud and scree) claim the title Chemin de Compostela here, I'm taking charge of navigation again.

- - - - -

Oh, joy! A new pain! Something completely different. See how I suffer to offer variety to my readers. Something somewhere in my abdomen suddenly feels fit to explode after I adjusted my pack (in the constant contest to lessen pain). Readjusting alleviated the problem, but not my doubts. Had I herniated my intestines, perforated an ulcer, or burst my appendix? Is that latter gland on the left or the right? Your left or my right? Does less pressure and pain only mean the explosion and aftershock have occurred? How long have I to live?

- - - - -

The pain has returned in full, as a sharp jab, making me sit down with a bump to unload the pack abruptly. The source of the conflict does not feel painful to the touch or lumpy. My pack not hanging properly on my back for weeks has probably caused the problem. My sole recourse now is to restore the load more gingerly, and to pray.

Heartfelt prayer seems to have done the trick. Without faith, as an agnostic, I always preached belief in personal experience alone; I can only preach the same now as a gnostic. My only advice: Look. See what you find.

Resuited for battle, but still quite lost in the dark, I immediately found the very road needed, along with a posted map confirming same. To a man worn to the bone, and weary to the soul, that's a miracle. Reaching the wee village of Montpeyroux, with unexpected speed, put me back on the official Chemin de Compostela. A park bench on the edge of town supplied all the rest of my needs, including all the rest needed.

Mon. 21/3/11

I was oddly relieved yesterday to find my sleeping bag wet again. I did not say I was oddly relieved and found my bed wet. I'm relieved no longer to suspect being targeted for a wet attack while asleep. Temperatures here fall farther than realized, or my bag fails in old age to keep-in heat, leading to dire condensation. Using a little blanket inside the bag may keep me warm and dry. The bag is flawed, but maybe I just grow colder as I grow older.

- - - - -

Montpeyroux looks like an odd little place, but I think I like it. I hung out all morning, while completing essential tasks. Had I known the path persisted so pleasantly out of town, I might have departed sooner. Wait 'til you view the stone bridge rebuilt for pilgrims, leading to la petite village perching above Montpeyroux. As is, the morning has fled without my going far. Locked and loaded, I left town as the church bell tolled the angelus, and the town clock told twelve. I tried and failed to explain (to a passing Frenchwoman) for whom the bell tolled: me.

I pray the angelus now, to honor my farmer father, though I can't really recall how he recited it in the fields. *Pour vous, mon pere.* Allow a second aside to family: Dear Jim, last night I dreamt you hike with me, out-hike me, and sans stick. To wake alone saddens me some, but I know I should be glad just to wake (as Dad used to tell us).

Under the heading of Pleasant Paths, include the climb over the mountain to St. Jean de la Blaquires, though I am not overly fond of winding inclines and declines now. St. Jean is a perfect destination for a perfect afternoon.

For the first time on this pilgrimage, a municipal refuge has signposted the way to cheap accommodation. I had hoped to spy more of that by now. Of course, you know I don't stop, though I've mislaid the path out of town.

No, I did ask for directions. Once you ask, you're obliged to follow even dubious instruction. I believe I've found the shortest route anyway. Let me mention here that road signs mean little in France. First, they are intended to direct drivers who don't care about a bit of extra distance. Second, the distances quoted can mislead. A passerby might see "20 km" posted to the next town, only to spot "22" after going 2 km. The problem is not a math problem. One sign might measure via that road to the edge of town, and the other by the autobahn to the heart of town, or vice versa, or worse, by some obsolete historic way.

I prefer the old-fashioned "milestones" because they measure in kilometers, not miles (much longer), to the town centers. Any hiker used to miles comes to food and shelter far faster than expected. Measurements on pilgrim signposts must mean even less in reality, but I felt glad to spy "1474 km" engraved in stone on the above bridge.

Whatever the distance, I tramped the road to Lodeve, landing a bit bumpily. Bummed out by my travails, I delighted to learn (according to a compostela factsheet) the hotel I happened to pass had a special rate for pelerins. The historic Hotel du Nord had already attracted my attention. Happily gaining entry, I found the new owners disallowed all discounts. I took the room regardless as the standard rate struck me as quite special, and the other info on my "factsheet" proved out-of-date too. One hospitaler had been dead for five years. Though I can't confirm my guidebook's opinion that the Hotel du Nord is "the best in the city," I would recommend it (especially in warmer weather) for the terraces and central location. The patisserie opposite may be the best in the province. Down the street, the local laundromat helpfully sits. The nearby cathedral and war memorial reward enough, in their uniqueness, to make worthwhile one visit to Lodeve.

Tues. 22/3/11

I just learned that I walked through an area yesterday that, due to uranium mining, possesses the highest surface radioactivity in the world. Glad I didn't camp there. Would not a little prior warning be appropriate? Of St. Martin du Bosc, the ville at the epicenter of radioactivity, I recalled the many children playing in the schoolyard as I passed by quite late. Now I wonder if that ground had been specially decontaminated.

Wicked muscle cramping (in the legs) woke me in the middle of the night, presumably not due to radioactivity. Fumes from a sewer plant had made me hold my breath while walking past. No warning again. How unfair of my muscles to remind me so painfully of my oxygen debt, as if they did not owe the lungs I saved. Mob debt-collectors would not have treated my poor legs harder.

My oxygen-robbed muscles could have used another warning today, about the mountains following Lodeve. Definitely the official Chemin de Compostela, the route swings wildly over a high mountain to Lunas. When I first surveyed the way, I coulda cried. I laughed instead as my pitiful hopes raised and fell at every big bend in the road.

The French have a terrible penchant for constructing high highways. Regarding a peak, a French engineer will ignore any convenient gap, or low shoulder, to swing right over the top, where naught waits, in order to create 5 or 10 km of unnecessary climbing. "Serpentine" wouldn't do to describe the resulting D35. Monstrously snakish, gargantuan-pythonesque (striking and constricting) better describes a road that nearly swallowed me whole.

How wise of me in retrospect not to press on to Lunas last night, though maps show it temptingly close. I'd have died on that mountain. In daylight the ordeal over to Lunas proves less than lunacy only because Lunas renders the trek worthwhile. But I wouldn't repeat it, though I'd love to hike again around the town. Next time, I'll take a bus to where this striking jewel sits fixed in its antique setting, warmly glowing in sunshine and hospitality.

- - - - -

I had not much time to enjoy that timeless place as an extra deadline had been added to my itinerary. The ideally located laundromat in Lodeve left me high and wet, because both of its dryers were busted. That put a sweaty climb between me and the next dryer in Bedarieux, and with the additional weight of wet gear. Add to that the psychological weight of a hard push to a laundry likely locked.

Reaching town around 7:00 p.m., typical closing time, I still needed time to find the laundromat. When I did, and pushed on the door, I chortled out loud when it opened. Relaxing in relief, I misread a sign, and nearly misled myself into misery. Believing I had loads of time to dry my load, I was totally surprised when the lights and dryer shut off—just as my clothes finished! In a huff, I packed up by emergency lighting, before the owner showed (with dogs) to lock up. Then the light dawned on me. Giggling again as doors locked behind me, I thanked Jesus for small mercies, and great salvation, before walking away into the night. No bed for me in Bedarieux.

At least my sleeping bag feels dry. In the town's outer limits a satellite traffic-circle orbits, displaying the golden arches. Too late to dine inside, my empty belly obtained a meal at the drive-thru counter, counter to policy. My cold bones McD's blessed unintentionally with discarded cardboard boxes (salvation of hobos). This extra insulation makes quite comfortable the bench in a nearby bus shelter.

- - - - -

While searching for this brief abode, I stopped to note the most remarkable difference between walking across Europe or America. Hiking here for two weeks, across two countries, I had not once been grilled by the police, or even noticed. In America, I could not walk 1 mile of 3,000 before being interrogated, an exercise repeated 100 times in every jurisdiction, city, county, state and federal. Oddly, the biggest controversy in the country then boiled over whether police should be granted power to ask any innocent passerby where he came from, where he went, who he was and what I.D. proved it. Objectors seek to keep guaranteed civil liberties we obviously have not got.

Even while writing, I felt the ink jinxing me. Sure enough, within minutes, the gendarmes arrived. When their vehicle whizzed by a dark bus shelter, sheltering a bum from most eyes, I just knew the coppers knew about me. Confirming the sharp rep of France's national paramilitary police force, the sound of an illegal U-turn came from down the street. Their SUV swept past to round the roundabout and break hard by where I lounged in my sleeping bag. As doors flew open, boyos in black jumpsuits (with matching guns) jumped out into shoot-out positions. A patently senior officer then says to me, "*Bonsoir*" only.

Holding up my clamshell symbol of St. James, I replied, "*Je suis un pelerin de St. Jacques.*"

Aside from a grave pause, the only police response was "OK" before they bundled back in, to drive away.

They never pressed me for a pilgrim passport, never mind my real one, which you know is not quite in order.

Boy, I feel bowled over, like they shot me with a stun gun. Having much experience with law enforcers, in New York and Northern Ireland too, I feel qualified to grant the Hobo Prize for Humanity (and common sense) to that officer. Unless you know the whole story of St. Roch, you won't fully grasp the significance of the officer's leniency. The saint died in prison rather than answer official interrogators other than, "*Je suis un pelerin de St. Jacques.*"

Though a famous miracle-working nobleman, he chose to remain an anonymous pilgrim to authority interfering with Le Chemin de St. Jacques. I must confess to you and

St. Roch, but not the cops, that I would have spilled my guts to the best of my ability had I been questioned, though, like Roch, I have endured plague and injury.

The gendarme probably just didn't desire to hear more of my fractured French. Regardless, though St. Roch knows I'm not like him, I got to play his part, while avoiding his fate miraculously. The pilgrim saint also gave me opportunity to care for a plague-ridden pilgrim in rainy Arles, but I was more concerned about contagion. Tsk!

- - - - -

Last night cramps grabbed me with such tearing force, I could swear me crippled. Yet, spasms disappear without effort or effect. During the day, I thought exertions had definitely damaged my left leg, and maybe they did, but pain has disappeared after I prayed over it. Call it mind over matter if you like, I still call it miraculous.

Wed. 23/3/11

The pelerin proved the policeman's good judgment by being underway before dawn, down the road towards Lamalou des Bains. Old railroad aqueduct arches provide a dramatic entrance to this wee berg. Townsfolk could try more to keep its streets special. Nature supplies the drama required to render special the next town, Columbieres, even if you don't arrive by the secret route I took. Look for yourself. Look for a lonely chapel on a mountain.

As fine as tree-lined lanes look to you drivers as you whiz through, pedestrians cannot much enjoy the view while playing hide and seek with lethal vehicles. To liven things up (or make them more lethal), plane trees drop down dead branches, like most trees shed leaves. Perhaps shoddy pruning is to blame, but these branches only play dead until they trip you into deadly traffic. Hence a pilgrim should search for alternative routes.

In the weeks past, I have twice wandered down trails only to land behind locked gates. Both times, luckily, no guards or guard dogs trapped me against the wire. Once an angry horse stamped and pawed behind me, while beehives hummed beside me. Yet I set off again today, cutting down the drive of a chateau because it appeared to curve back to the road before gates or guns might come into play. Appearances proved correct in this case.

Then, I took a path past a shack, and into an adventure, in the Kingdom of the River Ruler. If that sounds make-believe, don't believe less than real courage was required to come through. If you play the game correctly, you emerge from dark forest into a high, bright place, where a monument stands to fallen heroes. I would love to return to the valley of the Orb, Dept. of Herault, to explore at my leisure when God is not pushing me. Passing as a pilgrim, you can trust St. Roch (hint) to not lead you astray. He'll bring you to Mons la Trivalle, which isn't trivial, as a rails-to-trails begins there. That perfect path brings you all the way to Couriou, a full day's hike for most.

Darkness had already fallen on the town prior to Couriou—Olargue—causing me to consider halting there, where other advantages beckoned: a mega-market and possible accommodation. As you have doubtlessly noted by now though, I am a driven individual when walking. Well, I've seldom been made sorrier for that character flaw.

In twilight, my inspiring life-saving trail Jekylls into Murderers' Row. Switching from valley-spanning arcs, the erstwhile railroad cuts a deep channel through solid rock for a solid kilometer, suddenly sinking hikers into shadow. Not satisfied, fate throws in three unlit tunnels, and swooping bats (carriers of rabies on the continent).

God only knows what other killers lurk. This likely crime statistic found the hike to Couriou longer than daylight measurement indicates. When on arrival he found a church reaching out to him with an inviting pilgrim porch of old, complete with benches, the survivor felt compelled to pause for prayer. There lay his undoing, or salvation, when he lay down for a moment...

Thurs. 24/3/11

Though the church bell sounded hours and quarter hours, the weariest of men slept quite soundly until 5:00 a.m. and walked proudly before 5:30. Surprised to find the rail-trail continue past the posted terminus, I carried on, only to learn why Couriou claims to close the route. What waited was a walking/waking nightmare. Worse in daylight than last night's Murderers' Row, the Gates of Hell opened for me. Thanking Christ I never came on this in the black of night, I blundered or bulldozed onward. The initial warning, police tape flapping, I ignored. Whatever the danger ahead, it could hardly top a highway with no shoulder. Storms having washed out the path became too evident soon, but I struggled on until a tunnel mauwed.

How long it stretched I couldn't guess; I knew no lights worked and no light showed from the far end. My dimming penlight did not help to explain the sound of rushing water ahead or an unrecognized cry of an animal or lost soul. The possibility of rabid bats or larger hunters certainly lurked, insect, animal, human or inhuman. Impassible barriers, of construction or destruction, looked likely to bar progress or escape. Had I turned back yet though? Your footloose fool was soon swallowed into the black bowel of the beast.

Water fell so hard from the roof that the roof falling hard looked likely. Once the tunnel began to bend, relief at the explanation for no light ahead felt conditioned by the loss of light behind. On we tread, trying to avoid obvious showers from the ceiling and streams in the floor. Sadly, spoiling the suspense by writing this story, I survived. Excuse me for living. On emerging—at the run—from the tunnel, I felt relief flow unconditionally, but prematurely, as the current that rushed with me from the tunnel currently washes away the path there.

While the towns above Mons work at converting more of the disused railway to footway, let's hope the towns below Couriou labor to re-establish what they already have. Once the river reaches the latter area, most of the valley loses much of its charm, however, not just down the above drain, but by generally growing more industrial. Finally, an organic fertilizer factory bisects *la voie verte*. Organic or no, the factory does no favor for the olfactory. Though able to hook up afterwards with an auto-free trail, you won't find it as sweet as above Olargue.

Speaking of olfactory senses, the novel notion of building (maintaining and cleaning) public toilets looks increasingly foreign to France. I don't object to toilets for customers only, only to no toilets at all, or abominations.

Less than charming myself, I failed to return to a boulangerie in St. Anns to thank them for the best pizza eaten in Europe to date—real tomato pie. Don't darken the door of anyplace in France calling itself "Snack Bar."

Even less charming, ego forces old legs to move all the way to Castres in a day, to put my soul back onto *le route du pelerin*, within striking distance of Toulouse. I hope in fact to arrive in time to see Toulouse before today's deadline— through the clever device of an autobus. Don't worry, I haven't surrendered. *Au contraire*, I mean tomorrow to attempt again a half pack/double-hike, despite previous failure and two 50 km days on the trot.

While my brain remained bold and brassy, coming into Castres my legs turned to tin, and my own gut near gutted me. The route had been the harshest so far, the opposite of yesterday's freedom from infernal combustion. Regardless my feet arrived at the Le Gare Routiere before 8:00 p.m., expecting to find transport. When posted schedules and bystanders told me no, disappointment hit me hard, but not enough to drive me away. Doggedly hanging on, I noticed an empty bus come to life, and its signboard read "Toulouse" in light.

Though the coach would head in the opposite direction first, along the very road I'd near tragically trudged, it did eventually turn towards Toulouse, and for free for me, though possibly not intentionally. With the aid of my guide-book, I located an inexpensive hotel, ideally close to the station—despite my late arrival (The Ambassador). No one could have landed this plan better, even if making a second approach, and not just winging it.

CHAPTER 4
Toulouse to St. Jean Pied de Port, France

Fri. 25/3/11

Falling into deep sleep while watching French TV, I woke feeling unrested and unready try an 80-km day. So, I dedicated the day to ascertain how best to do 80 tomorrow, and to finding cheaper digs. The 6:45 bus and L'Auberge de Compostela fill the bill, despite the first requiring a 5:45 alarm, and the latter being a bit bogus as a pilgrim refuge. The hostel can claim a nice location for viewing the old town, but The Ambassador offers better exiting from town. Moving may cost me tomorrow.

Slightly staggering, I wander streets on different errands, while my bowels run in different directions, dehydrating me more before a long march. My condition may jaundice my view, but I don't care for Toulouse anymore, though we were once in love. Montpelier writ large, Toulouse proves bigger ain't better. Changed from how I knew her, a fate not her fault, *c'est dommage*. Never have I witnessed more open prostitution, public inebriation and urination—not even in New York's dark days. Ruination!

On the bright side, I have finally (after halfway) worked out how best to carry all my accoutrements. About time. My feet suddenly look their best since Milan!

Sat. 26/3/11

Without even employing an alarm clock, a valiant attempt at the early bus nearly did catch it. Toulouse so turns travelers in twisting medieval streets, I arrived at Le Gare Routiere just in time to watch the bus pull out. Even then, had I known which way to gallop to head 'em off at the pass, this cowboy coulda caught 'em. I bolted left, and wrong, not right. "There is a tide…" This voyager could feel his keel sinking into the mud. Having only to wait two hours for the next bus, I knew the delay would be far more, and more than dangerous. I never departed Castre until nearly noon. The town clock struck doom.

- - - - -

The most remarkable event of the day was the walk itself. 80 km by 1:30 a.m. sounds like boasting, but I merely report facts, and give credit to God. There goes another pilgrim rosary though. Number 4? Had I caught the earlier service, I'd have finished before the witching hour. As is, two more hours I required to reach my hostel bed. Along the route, Castres stood out at the outset. Surprisingly, this close to Toulouse, the town offers much, and refuses to let the larger neighbor suck it dry of culture and opportunity. The smaller berg even dares to challenge Toulouse for the same market day (today).

Plucky Owego, N.Y., on the Susquehanna River, reminds me of a similarly set Castres. Why not twin?

The final real town before Toulouse also stands out, particularly if passed after dark. Verfeil would've appealed more could I have held her before closing time. Even that late, some places stayed open, including a clean public loo! Knock me down with a feather and a fart! Precious to pilgrims.

Sun. 27/3/11

Of this day let me say, I am proud of escaping the grasping tendrils stretching out from Toulouse and ashamed to have missed Mass, however undeliberately. Indeed I'm especially embarrassed by the inadvertency. Showered and shaven, if unshriven, I face my fate: wrestlin' with the labyrinth of autobahns entangling Toulouse.

I even discovered the official chemin de St. Jacques, but only after deciding to forego that in favor of the D632 towards Lourdes. My ma would like anything from Lourdes, and my limbs may require miraculous healing.

Besides 80 km yesterday, I also completed the essential task of certifying the arrival of my postal package in St. Jean Pied de Port, plus the willingness of the post office to hold it till April 5th. That took some doin', even with the help of angels in Toulouse and Castres. The hike into the Pyrenees may prove hard but should hit the deadline handily enough. Don't even ask where I've landed at the moment though. Towns continue conjoinedly, keeping a hiker confused but on a clear path. Sidewalk like this to Lourdes would constitute a miracle for me. Damn if I'm not tired as hell however, and needing to lie down somewhere here in St. Wherever.

Mon. 28/3/11

Oh, oh! The property picked last night belongs to the Catholic Church, probably a good choice for a pilgrim, but the gendarmerie operates next door, their back door facing me. I peed practically on their property! Darkness would not shield me from infrared cameras. No repeat performance matinee-ed at least. As a bad omen, one of my shell symbols lay broken this morning. That looks to me like a warning.

I should mention that no public ground, and little private property, in all of France has not been peed upon by man and beast. The average Frenchman displays far less discretion than I. Indeed, traditional public toilets tend towards too public. Urinals in full view display other than discretion. Women don't hesitate to squat anywhere either. My intimate investigations of brushy areas reveal more about heavy drug use in this country than any need "to use the bushes."

From that town I hotfooted to the next, Fonsorbes, where I stop to view the interesting parish church and to have my pilgrim passport stamped. The authorities argued that their town did not figure in le route de pelerins, and I replied that it does now. Who would know better than a pilgrim? At the rear of the church, the view sweeps wide and handsome. The phrase might equally apply to the controversial statue standing in front of the church and Our Lady of Lourdes statue. Hoping the priest had nothing to do with the placement of the more modern work, I presume this art part of an apparently official effort to de-Catholicize France. Separating carnival from Mardi Gras (and Ash Wednesday) all across the country can't be coincidental.

Nothing remarkable about the next few villages, other than the pastry shops permitting me to surpass my hiking goal for the day: Lombez. Samatan/Lombez look very traditional, but forward looking, and between them they provide for pilgrims a dream trail. Though very pleasant to reach at the close of day, the good-going path only pushed me harder to reach Lombez before everything closed. Though beating my expected speed, I still came too late because I crossed an unexpected time zone or daylight-saving jump. (Hey, maybe that's why I missed Mass.)

By God's grace one pizza shop had yet to close. Though I did not expect much of last-minute pizza, "Good Pizza" Restaurant lives up to its English name, and the place matched its product in quality. I could not have been more blessed had I all the time on the clock. I'd love to return to Samatan and Lombez with more time.

Only one thing bugged me about the latter town. En route I would enquire, "*Quelle distance a Lombez?*" pronouncing the name with a "long A" ending, according to the rules of French taught to me. Always the response came, "*Je ne sais pas*" (I don't know) followed by, "Oh, you mean Lombeeze," or sometimes "Lombess." Shut up.

From Lombessybeezia I lurched onward alone, only looking for a likely stopping place. A dozen presented, only to disqualify as too private private property, or too public public-property. The path, now unlit, took me toward the next town's lights—I thought. A very fancy chateau, down a lighted lane, offered a lit-up restaurant for gourmets, but nothing for poor pelerins. Miles farther from town, an old hay barn silhouetted against the sky. "Too private," I reckoned, but erected my tent in the field next to it, as I'd have preferred if I owned the barn.

(P.S.: Again today, the enemy tried to stop me from taking a bridge by catching me in a pincer movement of heavy transport. When that happens, nothing brings up the knees better than the "U.S. Marine Hymn." Though I have no time for militaristic imperialism, and generally prefer Irish rebel tunes when on campaign, if my life depends on taking an objective, I put a D.I. in my head. I'm sure the French Foreign Legion has something suitable too, especially for a long march in boiling heat. As I don't know any, I'll have to write one myself.)

Tues. 29/3/11

Following the golden rule last night meant a wet tent delayed me this morning. My sleeping bag managed to find a little puddle besides. Morning nearly left without me for Boulogne-sur-Gesse. Had I known the town, I'd have walked my dawgs more diligently. Instead I dawdled, feeling so at home, not just because the farmer failed to eject me from his field. (Maybe his dog had run off and his ammo run out.) The surrounding countryside reminding me of Ireland (Co. Down's rolling drumlins) did affect my feelings but didn't effect them, though soil here seems heavier, stickier, furrowed sky above plowed earth, tied by light threads of rain, bespeaks a climate near the same, as does wild growth too. I even spotted gorse, of course. What puts me most at ease in this countryside is a sudden realization on the road last night: a tramp is a foreigner everywhere but on a road to anywhere. Fears faced in France scarcely differ from those felt in America or Ireland, etc.

- - - - -

About 20 km before Boulogne on the D632, travelers come across a crossroads tavern, of the type once common in France and Ireland. The quality of the establishment immediately evident, I called a halt for food, rest, and restroom. Learning what was served to me, I feared the last might follow the first without rest between.

Any pelerin de St. Jacques would feel obliged to try pizza named after the patron of pilgrims, though the key ingredient, noix de St. Jacques (nuts of St. James), made him uneasy, as it would most men (especially St. James).

Once tasted, the nuts made me think my entire system could soon be rendered more than uneasy. Nuts! Was I nuts to eat unknown nuts? Frenchmen eat anything! A fishy taste suggested something fishier than fish. Ever hear of "prairie oysters"? Of course, I held the answer to my urgent query all along. To be exact, it hung around my neck: a mollusk shell, the symbol of St. James. Truth did not set me free, or knowledge reassure. Knowing I had ingested foreign shellfish only unsettled my mind further, if not my stomach.

The dish tasted delish, however, and I recommend the restaurant, if not that unfortunately titled item. I can't recall the name of the establishment, but there's no other about. Never thought I would miss all of America's greasy spoon diners. France offers nothing comparable, particularly nothing open 24 hours. Many gas stations only open 24/7 because they're totally automated. Try finding a manned station, never mind one with a shop or toilet. Even most bars, which once served pub grub, don't bother anymore.

Reaching Boulogne sooner would probably only have meant my rushing past anyway. Arriving, when I did, made me wander the town to look for accommodation. A sprawling Irish market town came to mind, but few of those provide a campground and waterpark on the outskirts. I wouldn't mind coming here again, possibly with someone who would enjoy it more than me. Then, I could enjoy their enjoyment. Unfortunately for me, for now, camping is closed, making me wander and wonder more. A lonely park bench (under lights shut off or put out) has accepted me. No tent appears needed, as every star in the sky lights my bed.

12:15 a.m., Wed. 30/3/11

My day starts early, and disastrously. I did declare that weather near the Pyrenees acts like the drunkenly changeable Irish variety. However, not even in Erin has a sky ever gone from completely cloudless to entirely blanketed and wet in two windless hours. Trying to write without showing a light, I dozed off with my head inside my sleeping bag, and slept unsuspecting, to wake with a terrible start, for no reason but the grace of God...

Sticking out my head like a turtle, I faced the first sprinkle and raced into action like a hare. Out from my pack the tent flew to cover my body, while my umbrella sprang to defend my head and pillow/pack. Knowing disaster would flow from anything more than a brief shower, I hoped for the best, but got five hours of steady rain. My worry, that a cold drenching would prevent needed sleep, prevented sleep.

To doze (or wake with a start) might mean movement that unleashed a flood (from puddles formed in my crumpled tent), or spilled an umbrella, or extended a sleeping bag into a deluge. A fit of shivering would result, in a futile attempt to restore body heat. Illness would inevitably follow to terminate my pilgrimage at the very least. Worse, precious belongings carried from America, and across half of Europe, faced ruin—not least this journal.

Only after my fifth pilgrim rosary in as many weeks did the downpour let up, but in the dark, all movement or slumber remained perilous. Only after 7:00 a.m. could I peel back the tent painstakingly, to check for damages. Miraculously, only two items, already ready for discarding, landed in the bin. At peace, I slipped into sleep.

- - - - -

The rest of the morning that resting left, drying-out occupied. That did not preclude more sightseeing and shopping in Boulogne. Can't call the morning wasted. Though tardy departing for Tarbe, I do feel confident in reaching there, especially as my hand now clutches a detailed map, thanks to the quality of Boulogne merchants. They also inform me that Elizabeth Taylor has died—two days ago.

My new map permitted me to leave the traffic of the main road and to view French rural life from a closer perspective. The different traffic discovered did not delight. First, you will inevitably come to a narrow stretch of road approaching the main road, where everyone going to or from anywhere turns off or onto the pike. Dangereux, but worse awaits. Just as I switched from one slim route to a slighter one, an ATV roared down on me, with two large dogs roaring louder. Silently I picked up two stones.

When the poltroon pulled up to grin dopily, his dogs also showed their teeth, while more dogs raced up the lane on the left to join the fun. An open gateway on the right also emitted demented barking. With nowhere to go but back, I stepped forward, staff raised, to direct the driver down the lane to meet his pack. Not smiling, I tried to communicate seriousness. Convinced, he roared away with his howling hounds.

I'm convinced that an alarming canine progression occurs across Europe. In Italy any walker will be greeted by a cacophony like feeding time at a kennel. Not very welcoming. However, invariably the yelping emanates from behind well-maintained fences. In France the decibels lessen somewhat, but more dogs wander out and about, often unleashed, to leave dogshit everywhere. Spain spills out loose mutts, in a large variety of large varieties. No dog can I recall ruining my day in Croatia or Bosnia. Go figure.

Scarier than canines, the gleaming white teeth of the Pyrenees, my primary destination, are bared outside Boulogne. Am I insane? Don't answer that. I am not afraid though, as I have come to expect miracles as required.

I may expect too much as I probably just poisoned myself. Trying to take it easy today, after a trying night, I only hiked to Castelnau, in some heat. No castle noted, I did spy a supermarket and decided to obtain a proper meal. As a rule, avoid rotisserie chicken here, as butchers load raw birds above nearly done ones before handling cooked poultry. However, today two overcooked leftovers looked OK, until I witnessed the butcher paw raw cuts for the customer before me. Turning away immediately, I heard the butcher, or the grim reaper, call after me…

Thinking quickly, I asked a question ever answered negatively to date, "Can I buy a part of that chicken?"

"No," he replied; I played disappointed.

Damn if he didn't call me back again.

Contaminated fingers snatched a bird and chopped with a dubious knife on a more dubious block.

Oh, he had wiped his hands on his pants first. Then he charged me for extra labor. If disappointment had felt difficult to fake, delight proved harder.

I confess to having discarded sausage bought from another butcher of hygiene. Replacing that sausage in a shop selling only cooked meats, I threw away that purchase in turn, for its dodgy texture and taste. However, I had no intention of wasting an expensive half chicken. Besides, the dubious meat removed all doubt about renting a room in Castelnau. If not chicken of the chicken, I feared traveling far from a private loo. Last night's hard camp had left me gun-shy. Good thing it did, as in my room my sleeping bag revealed how wet it still remained. Lying down on cold ground in a damp bag? Definitely dangerous. Socks and underwear require washing and careful drying anyway, not to mention myself.

I wish, after such service, I could recommend L'Hotel Dupont, a Victorian relic rising on the main square, but I can't. However, doesn't wishing I could commend it say something positive about the place? I believe the dining excellent, but had no opportunity to confirm that personally. Despite no castle standing where one should, I do praise the town for its unusual architecture. More Alpine, Bavarian even, than anything spotted around here, the buildings were perhaps intended to make foreigners feel at home, more than express any notion innate to the area.

Thurs. 31/3/11

If I am poisoned, the agent is not violently fast-acting. That's good, I guess. Yet I'm slow to leave my hotel. My money's worth needs to be fully gleaned. Anyone who sleeps rough should treasure a bed.

Today I spy the first of the big vultures who follow pilgrims through the Pyrenees. He would be wise to keep his beady eyes on me.

- - - - -

Despite my late start, I set out determined to attain Tarbes today, to remain on schedule. My boiler stoked, I did not let up till hitting Tarbes, a big dull place, with nothing open to reward my effort. One restaurant which refused to serve a latecomer did part with a liter of water—at four times the proper price. That's shocking to a pelerin de St. Jacques. This pilgrim felt pleased and blessed to get it though. Washing down some scraps still carried, essential hydration enabled my body to chug on through town to the Tarbes-Lourdes Airport, a fair distance even if you have not already hiked from Castelnau, or from Italy.

Where I hoped to find comfort, however, I found locked doors. An unusually comfortable bus shelter does stand nearby. Airport facilities will open in a few hours (my watch says 2:00 a.m. now). Tomorrow, after I take care of some business there, and "take care of business," a final push will put me in Lourdes reasonably early.

P.S.: I did not rush through the countryside too fast to enjoy surrounding rustic architecture. Mixed adobe and stone (topped by tiles) ties together home and barn. Looks almost legally required. I like the look and the effort to maintain it. Personally, I reckon the climate too damp to suit, and the state of many buildings confirms my opinion. Little churches with large porches also charm this pilgrim.

Fri. 1/4/11

Observing the ads at the airport, "Fly Cheap from Milan to Lourdes," I had to laugh. Like now they tell me!

Only through the Christian kindness of airport service workers was I able to book with Ryanair (not the flight desired) from Santiago to Stansted, England, at double the advertised price. Never again with Ryanair.

Once outside the airport, I discovered God's little practical joke on me. Atremble for days at the thought of shivering in my final frigid approach into the icy Pyrenees, I swelter instead on the hottest day to date. I'm not laughing. Though I know God is All-good, humor must remain a matter of personal taste. If at the Pearly Gates we're informed He only kidded about the Ten Commandments, I won't be surprised—and I won't be laughing.

Lourdes thinks it funny to direct dehydrated pilgrims, along with auto traffic, an extra 2 km to the city center. Once in, pedestrians find *petite* signposts and painted paths to direct them—too late. Lourdes looks a small city now, quite built up on the backs of invalids, and I felt ready to dislike it. However, the magic took hold once more, and I left things to do should my legs ever carry me back. Considering the amount of blessed water with which a limping pilgrim doused himself, he should live long enough to return, or to regret not doing so.

Stress kills me now. Walking best cures that, unless walking provides the stress. Deadlines march on me, one after the other, bound to slay me eventually. Lourdes attained, stress lessens generally, and produces a plan to reduce it further. I will leave here by train to Pau tonight, to return tomorrow to hike back. Abruptly new deadlines appear, as Lourdes oddly expects much tramping by pilgrims, as does a mother of her son. I do my duty.

Sat. 2/4/11

Boy, what a mistake! Trying to be clever, I exited a famous tourist trap to seek accommodation in a city of considerable reputation. However, Lourdes holds more hotel space than anywhere outside Paris. Warned much would have closed, due to new laws, I did not expect to find hordes of bargains going begging, but I did—too late. As you may have noticed by now, I'm not much for turning. All to do done by 8:45 p.m., I caught my train.

Traveling very off-season, I'd yet to experience any difficulty over availability of accommodation. In Pau God delivered the desired hotel again, but the devil delivered a sting in the tail.

By merest chance—or miracle—I enquired about leaving my pack tomorrow. Asking from politeness, I expected the customary "*Certainment*," but heard "*Non*."

Quelle surprise! The hotel would close the next day for renovation. Fresh good fortune soured in a second. Locating my second-choice hotel in minutes, I found it full, and time running out. Luckily spotting another two-star hotel with a night-clerk still on, I learned a last-minute non-negotiable price might break me. The clerk did tell me of competition around the corner, where poorer location meant possibly accepting poor pilgrims. That Christian kindness broke the chain of *malchance*.

L' Hotel Bosquet (Rue Valery Meunier 05 59 11 50 11) appeared as an answer to prayer and provided more than required at a price just a touch above budget. The hotel deserves a third star. Sometimes the weary do need more than they need. Y'know what I mean? Finding this bargain without the aid of a guide particularly pleased me.

- - - - -

That presented again the problem of gleaning full value for money, which meant not leaving my room until after 9:30 a.m., in time to cadge the last train before 10:00 to Lourdes, 40 km away. I'd have caught the train too, had it ever run when I ran, on Saturdays. Oh well, another service showed up without making me wait too long, to put me in Lourdes before 11:00, with a few things still to do—practical and religious. The bells of the Shrine banished me by noon, but geared up again before the city finally let me go. Ironically, Lourdes water, for which the world comes, costs nothing; but beware the price of ordinary bottled water. An important point to note: Lourdes is now a recognized starting point for pelerins de St. Jacques.

The march between Lourdes and Pau, comparatively nondescript, still contains several points of interest (not including pastry shops) that might dangerously delay a proper pilgrim. Points of steeples especially interest me, as little villages once contested each other in ecclesiastic edifices. Extra points for originality? Of course, Lourdes would go overboard by building four churches on top of each other. Other towns didn't want to play anymore.

If you cross the river on the intended pilgrim route, a memorable monastery (St. Michael's) waits, plus, just a piece farther, a parish church in a town whose name I can't recall, but which also offers food shops.

Let me point out that despite a late start and many distractions I reached sidewalks and streetlights before full nightfall did. That's particularly fortunate as I needed to ride the road barrier one more time on a twisting mountain road. That makes once in the Alps, once in the Maritime Alps, and once in the Pyrenees. I quit at lucky three.

Nevertheless, by the time I relocated my hotel, and dined again on pizza, bells tolled twelve to urge me onto the road again. I took my time exiting Pau though, as she deserves attention. I'm pleased to announce I'd be pleased to return to her. Pau advertised its mountain air "for the cure" in Protestant England, long before Papists heard of Lourdes water. A free fun funicular from le gare to the public promenade, besides easing consumptive lungs, puts the entire city on a pedestal from where the view alone could cure all but the blind. Pau does seem to lack a bit of something that vibrant Montpelier possesses, but this ville on a hill has not caught whatever louses up Toulouse.

P.S.: The Brits brought rugby with them a century ago. Now you'd swear no other game exists on the planet.

Sun. 3/4/11

If Pau is easier to leave than Toulouse, that's a compliment to Pau. The task takes long enough nonetheless; even "to take" Laroin took a lot out of me. This town I discovered already occupied by genuine gypsies. Seeking a safe place to sleep, I'd decided to move on (because real gypsies stayed put), when a carload of coppers swooped…

Once again, my pilgrim badge spared me all questioning, though I trespassed on council property!

Discretion dictated pushing past Loroin to Argue Love (Artigue Louve) where a lawn in a business park looked mighty comfortable, especially as Sunday should let me sleep-in. Typically pushing my luck two minutes too far, I let two private police catch me. For the third time, my pelerin badge shielded me! True, I looked harmless, quite innocently guilty, and obviously leaving already, but the badge did the trick, saying more than I could, even in English. In my defense, I'd have been long away had not God sent rain on a Sunday morning. I don't complain, as rain came kindly to allow a sleep-in when workers weren't due. Up in time for any likely Mass locally, I would learn as morning passed, my sole hope lay in an evening service in a large town. I would have you know, as God knows, I went out of my way to try several churches before Mourenx, until I had to run to get there "in time."

Prior to Mourenx, a more temporal hell threatened and pushed me. In the morning though, I took my time, pausing in Arbus at a village rummage sale, where one woman (of a New Age gypsy kind) kindly offered un pelerin a bowl of soup. Hesitantly if happily accepting, I wolfed the steaming mix of meat and veg. Duck dominated, the best cuisine consumed since Milan. Grateful for anything besides pizza, I praised the cook, with no dissembling.

To where has the legendary cuisine of Belle France disappeared? To nowhere in my price range. "Pizza" becomes the commonest word in the French language.

Between Arbus and Abos, a hamlet of no name sits cut off from the world by a highway bypassing it. The roadblock bandaging the severed route into town cannot block a hiker from visiting a chapel of such quaint form it compels him to stop, if only to ask forgiveness for missing Mass. God welcomes me with open arms, embraces me with a big pilgrim porch. Spending the night would suit; instead I suit up before stepping back into pouring rain...

- - - - -

By timely gifts of pilgrim porches, by the passover of grim deluges, by the free pass granted me by police, pillocks, and psychos, by shops held open for me, by McDonald's appearing precisely when needed, I begin to feel specially blessed; but my biggest deliverance came today as I approached the edge of Monein. A petrochemical plant squats there, as ugly as you can possibly imagine, belching worse than you could imagine—not from its tall stacks but from every low valve or cracked pipe. The wind taking this noxious cloud away from me appeared to shift precisely as the road turned towards the monstrous mill. I knew the Almighty would understand if I stopped stopping to check churches. Heels hit the road hard, as a jig played in my head. At a fair clip I passed that town before the plant poisoned it for the umpteenth time. One place in France you could not pay me to live.

Rain began to fall again (with God knows what in it), and heaven sent no Mass to meet me in Mourenx but did provide a McDonald's in which to dry out and let water out.

When rain ran out, I ran out, but the rain only played me. Like a judgment of God a downpour continued all the way to Navarrenx—many miles and hours later on a cold dark night. Too late I realized that my poncho ceased to cover my pouch of precious belongings.

Desperate to reach anywhere dry, I powered up endless hills to run down far slopes. Navarrenx ran from me, but at 11:30 p.m. I caught the minx, who then offered an open door to the community refuge. At this GiteCommunale, the first on this Camino, I coulda cried were I not dehydrated and soaking wet. As all beds appeared reserved, and no staff appeared, I bedded down on kitchen benches and hoped to disturb no one who might disturb me. Sssh!

Mon. 4/4/11

Navarrenx disappointed at first. Due to a description read, my bleary eyes desperately peered through the rain for a walled city on a well-lit hill. Instead, this bashful berg hid in a valley, behind unimpressive disintegrating walls. What I failed to realize, until leaving this morning, had I come from the other direction I would have found the promised martial showpiece. Approaching up the valley, you do face an impressively walled and gated town on a bluff above the river. In daylight I take time to enjoy exploring, dooming myself to another long night march.

I took occasion to fittingly fight a petite battle. My Irish blood was up, even prior to learning the town had raised its defenses against William of Orange. My emerging clumsily with all my gear from the gite's doorway inadvertently forced a small schoolboy to detour around me. Angry barking awoke me from preoccupation to see the boy back away from a snapping brute. When I stepped around the corner with my stick, the canine coward quit quickly. In a corner shop I bought a Bounty bar to eat with pineapple yogurt, a truly tropical treat, and fair reward.

Finally, I'm meeting pilgrims on camino, and one just passed me. Better start heading if I'm to catch him.

Tues. 5/4/11

Even had I started earlier, darkness would have caught me. I don't want to say how hard this hike hit, as reporting from St. Jean means bragging, or begging for pity. Maps don't generally warn adequately of steep and narrow mountain roads, or of traffic on them. I am obliged to warn readers that the way went awfully hard, but I did sway into St. Jean in the wee hours. The post office had promised to hold my package until April 5th; I promised to be waiting when the doors opened. I was there, as was my reward—like I died and went to heaven. Incidentally, the views from the mountain Monday mimic heaven, but I could call the climb almost hellish.

The way looks like Ireland in a second way: sheep. Two hundred head headed across the road, just behind me, thank God. One more deliverance. Pyrenean sheep dogs don't look a patch on border collies. If the Pyrenean is cleverly bred to resemble sheep, possibly their brains look sheepish too. Bilingual signs also recall Erin, and not pleasantly.

From the St. Jean post office I repaired directly to the office of pilgrims, and the famous hostel opposite. The office of tourism and two tourist sites I took in too, before collapsing on my bunk bed. Rising before supper, I first squeezed in the last supper's re-enactment at Our Lady's Chapel down the street by the Pilgrim Gate. All pilgrims present received a special benediction and blessing.

CHAPTER 5
St. Jean, France, to Pamplona, Spain

Wed. 6/4/11

Today I declare a day for rest and contemplation (besides chores like laundry). Someone left lying atop a washer €5.00 in coin, the cost of a wash. After waiting to ascertain if anyone would return for the cash, I thanked God for whomever left the handy sum, especially if on purpose for a pilgrim. In turn I tried my best to aid a young man at the hostel who has backpacked about as far as I, but at far more cost to his aching body. I gifted him small items that might help, plus all the free advice I carried. First, "There's nothing you need more than you need less." You should have seen the things he'd lugged across France!

His pal, a German gal from Texas, discussed philosophy with me in a neat wee nook and bought my book. For that I will remain forever grateful, if only for not needing to carry that copy farther. She too arrives in St. Jean at the heel of a long hike and the head of another. She pauses here like me, but, unlike me, did not limp in at 4:00 a.m.

Even in the dead of night, proper pilgrimage I managed. When a sign promised a cross of note for pilgrims, my soul said, "Find it." Kind fortune, or benevolent Providence, placed the cross near the road. I can't swear how much more

I'd have lurched. I don't know either the full significance of said crucifix. Obviously of ancient origin, it looked a unique original. Whether due to great art or bad I don't know, but the artist presented to my eye the Child Jesus crucified, precisely what Mary must have seen on Calvary.

Then I considered the countryside crossed from Italy, chockablock with roadside crucifixes and cross-topped churches from whose steeples bells tolled the passing hours, and told the passing of the culture that had created them. Maybe that's one reason why some locals look kindly on passing pilgrims. We belong to the legion of the rearguard for their lost culture.

On a lighter note, before we leave France, let's have more fun with the language. Boldly advertised on shop fronts, "Traiteur, Bigot, Fagoterie, Die," attracts customers?! Not knowing what these words mean in French, I don't want to know, as I enjoy my ignorance too much.

- - - - -

As for the personal condition of this pilgrim, I felt pretty beat up approaching town, but feel upbeat now. Adrenaline flows on attaining my goal. Knowing I need rest, I am almost afraid to relax for fear of letting down my guard against the powers of darkness pursuing me. Do I dare to wind down whatever energy has driven me this far?

- - - - -

Advice to pilgrims: Start in Arles as you're meant to do, about a week later than I passed through, though I'd prefer Montpelier for St. Paddy's Day. The latter fancies itself the equal of Santiago, Rome, and Jerusalem on the medieval pilgrim route. That may say more about Montpelier than they want told. Starting in Arles March 23rd should put you at the Pyrenees for the last week in April, not the first, and let you finish in May, before high season and high heat.

Thurs. 7/4/11

Now the big day comes, to restart pilgrimage in the next exciting, difficult phase. Headin' over the hump, through the high pass to Roncevaux, none of us pilgrims will enjoy an easy romp. With errands to run in town—post office, Internet café, plus duties of a pilgrim (and a son) at the Church of Our Lady Our Mother—I failed to start with other devotees. Candles lit, I lit out through the Pilgrim and Spanish Gates, singing "Kelly the Boy from Killan," of course. Am I nervous? Guess so. Has my body recovered enough, or will it snap on the mountain like a dry twig?

- - - - -

As my answer, I can report feeling fine as I power past all pilgrims, including myself, as I revisit landmark rest stops of my previous Camino. Breezing by, I recognize the chestnut tree "planted by Charlemagne," where lungs gasped four years ago. Caution suggests rest today, as the steepest climb follows, but I feel pumped. The Orrison auberge looks better than recalled, but I only pause to say bonjour and to refill water bottles.

I did halt to help a damsel in distress, a local woman trying to load a lawnmower into a van, and did not fail to share my lunch with other pilgrims, while noting their names and nationalities. To them and others passed, I offer encouragement from my previous Camino experience. I take time to note the sweeping scenery that still reminds me of green Erin. I can appreciate also great improvements in the trail.

Cut stone markers and tall snow-stakes lead to a top-notch emergency shelter in the top notch of Roncevaux Pass. I delight in noting it not needed by me. Not only does no snow fall, underfoot looks warmer and dryer than in the fall of '07. My legionnaire anthem progresses nicely too. "*Bon courage, mes amis et Rose Marie*" matches the odd cadence required by marching feet in this heat.

Boldly bounding up the slope, I met a woman resting at the top who declared admiringly, "I can see you've climbed mountains before." That filly's comment made up for wild horses spoiling Roland's spring for me, leaving me short of water. Though her beau walked with her, I stopped to wrangle horses long enough for her to get water.

- - - - -

I would come running into legendary Roncevaux Abbey, in under eight hours from St. Jean, quite the quick jump, and just in time for Mass, showering, re-sewing and settling in.

Instead, I set off back up the mountain on a fool's errand: rescuing someone who looked in dire need but who never needed my help to come down by another route, while I climbed for an hour looking for him, before running down the steep path in the dark, for the second time in two hours (under full pack or half pack). No, I do not feel so hot now, and if any other wayfarer wants my help on this camino, he could carry on wanting.

Fri. 8/4/11

If I feel a bit broken today, that could be because God "busted" me. He regarded my motives in going back for the old Japanese fellow as less than pure. Can I help it? I did consider beforehand the truth about my altruism but decided anyone should do the right thing regardless. Hear my advice to any hiker now: *"Never go back."*

I should just have reported to the hostel keepers that an old man looked like he would die on the mountain. Let them send a vehicle to fetch him, with folks more rested and knowledgeable than me, not worried about curfew.

Wanting to play the hero, I acted the fool and may have doomed my Camino in my first hour in Spain. The Jap jagged right above the abbey, descending past the historic battleground of Roncevaux, where vain Roland met fate. The official trail once passed that way. A wise man from the east turned west because he knew the easier way. I'd understood that he had *not* caminoed already, or I would not have troubled to go back for him.

You find me today on a bus to Pamplona, the closest city along the Camino. Don't think you've busted me. I do recover from yesterday's ordeal, but I will return tonight to hike the way tomorrow. Today I will post ASAP all excess baggage to Santiago (seven kilos for seven Euros). Most importantly, the mailman will carry my tent, as the proper Camino provides regular pilgrim hostels at extremely low rates.

Once in Pamplona, I can check out accommodation for tomorrow when I'll arrive after a two-day hike for most peregrinoes. Tonight, the bus will take me back to enjoy all I missed in Roncevaux last night. Before that, I must finish most sightseeing in Pamplona, as I'll arrive late tomorrow and leave early the next day. Recalling the dramatically walled ancient capital of Basque country, I know it deserves more time, but far-off Santiago calls.

Sat. 9/4/11, Roncevaux to Pamplona

The most remarkable sight on today's trail surprises: little caterpillars. Though scarcely an inch long, on first sight I thought someone had lost a shoelace, as the wee wonders gather in long strings of 25 to 100. They may fool predators into thinking them a snake. Well they get busted and "busted" when cycling clubs rip down the path. Beware, as I hear they're extremely noxious—worms and cyclists.

A stranger, larger caterpillar crawls across the landscape. A young Spanish woman pushes a double stroller, followed by her husband pulling a heavily laden cart. The rocky route bounces the bawling babies, disturbing the peace of nature. An Irish lullaby shut them right up however, and an Irish donkey helped carry the baby buggy over the roughest ground. I offered to take photos too, to prove to kids (when grown) the truth of a family legend, perhaps when parents want pushed in wheelchairs to Santiago.

Most of today's route falls into the category of favored camino, traversing quaint historic towns and wooded hills by shady paths. Pleasant but still challenging, the trail receives testimony in stone from a monument placed on it. A memorial informs passing pilgrims that an elderly Japanese gentleman died here. Did anyone go back for him? Quite a coincidence; my seeing this marker here.

The way in and out of Zubiri I recall (to the excellent hostel too). More remarkably, the hostel mistress remembers me. Most surprising today is the effect my vigorous and confident persona seems to have on women. Long past Zubiri, when looking for directions from people picnicking, I boasted a bit about distance done and still to do, concluding, "Not bad for an old man," to which a very pretty young lady replied with a smile, "Not so old I think." At the hostel, an extremely attractive Englishwoman who admired my hiking today chose to chat by my bunk with her hand on my knee. An accomplished Swedish girl in the next bunk asks me to guide her from town tomorrow, an unnecessary task in Pamplona. Perhaps they know I'm harmless. Though "not so old," I am too old, too long in the tooth. Too bad.

Just past Zubiri waits the worst stretch of the Camino, across a wasteland that can waste you. Surrounding a satanic asphalt mill, the scarred landscape also deceives the unwary wayfarer made lightheaded by noxious fumes.

Though Zubiri's hostel keeper remembered me from four years ago, Pamplona's forgot me from yesterday. Despite my hurrying from Roncevaux (departing after 8:15 a.m. to arrive before 7:45 p.m.), the desired hostel had filled, pushing me to the large municipal albergue. Aside from noteworthy history, very few big advantages attend the bigger building, with its small shared (male/female) "facilities." Some small bonuses are also shared, but the biggest plus for me lay in meeting many of the people who had left St. Jean long before I, even the day before.

Hiker's Tip: Don't concern yourself overly with carrying provisions. Food you will find along the way. An unexpectedly good shop waits patiently at the far end of Gerendiain, the village before Zubiri. The region between there and the abbey has a history of witch trials two centuries ago. A black cat crossing my path at the shop caused me to take a wrong turn. Only time already lost prevented me from taking time to burn someone. Beware that cat, and the sharp left missed. Witchcraft might explain other ill-marked turns in this first stage of El Camino in Spain.

CHAPTER 6
Pamplona (Euskadi) to Santo Domingo, Spain

Sun. 10/4/11

Pamplona to Lorca. From Pamplona's albergue I departed before full daylight with the sweet young Swede. I left singing, as is my custom, and impressed one passerby at least, who insisted on bestowing a silver shell symbol of St. James. Genuinely grateful, I accepted less than graciously as the giver gave me an uneasy feeling.

Escaping my benefactor at that early hour left me dizzy enough to abandon my precious staff in a bakery. The real fault lay with bakery staff, distracting me by deliberately laying my naked baguette on the bare counter where customers lay hands, cash, coughs and sneezes! If leaving my stick did not impress the filly from Sweden, my galloping back, under pack to the bakery and back, did. All dashing done to no purpose, I would undashingly abandon her with new companions on the first hard climb, where we mutually decided I dashed too much—dash it! She'd have appreciated my dashing at wind-mills atop the ridge, in the tradition of Don Q, but with a hickory stick. Those titans pleaded for mercy, granted only after they pledged to employ their power to benefit the people.

Pilgrims pass at that highpoint a famous metal cutout of past pilgrims, reminding me of pilgrims passed before or *befour*. I don't miss pain suffered then, but it endeared others to me. I'll never walk alone on the Camino.

The church in Obanos laid claim to memory when passed purposely at Mass time. I recall desiring, when not a Mass-goer, to enter that church when locked. Mission accomplished years later, and mortal sin avoided, I've let past now all pilgrims passed. A fine wee grocery behind the church opens today just to delay me more.

Puente la Reina, a market town named for its royal bridge, serves as a civilized halting place, providing good accommodation and board (not boredom). I did stop in ancient chapels and inns but arrived too soon to stay. As forecasts knell grim for pilgrims, most stay. We'll see if I make the next town before the way's washed away.

- - - - -

Ciranqui, recollected fondly from befour (sic), still stands with great dignity above the plain. At the peak of the village an ancient steeple peeps out at approaching pilgrims. With a little running, this walker won the race to sheltering archways before the lash of rain did more than sting. Having missed with a wide swing, the downpour swept off, seeking defenseless wanderers, unaware that one followed close. Due to the fearsome rep of this storm, I walked alone from regal bridge to Lorca. Let this lesson all who would follow me. Ignore forecasts (of hard climbs too). Do what you can do on the day. Do no more. Hostels pop up frequently to render serious planning superfluous, and not a little silly. I'd have appreciated a warning about the sewage plant, the chemical factory and the open landfill en route. This wanderer might have tried another route, while wondering what the locals try to say to us.

Capturing Lorca, I considered campaigning to Villafuerta, but God, just outside two albergues, sprinkled me kindly. Taking that as a sign, I turned into the open door of the cheaper refuge on the right. Hospitality more than compensated for shortcomings in the building itself. Lorca surprises too with a nice deli at the far end of town.

Mon. 11/4/11

Exiting Lorca after 10:00 a.m. I do appreciate God's direction to halt where I did, but the rain never did reign hard enough to rein me in. See what I mean about forecasts?

Estella I find as remembered. Medieval churches still pose strikingly above streets with attractive shops. The path into town appears improved, as I recall falling on my face there. No, I wasn't drunk. The famous fountain dispensing free wine sits on the far side of Estella. Though teetotal myself, I stop to point out free refreshment to other pilgrims. Just past there I find refreshment in the face of a very pleasant oriental girl from Vancouver. Though she sits nursing her feet, she smiles only slightly less readily than in St. Jean. I pray the path treats her feet more pleasantly, the daintiest wee feet ever seen on a grown woman. Advice and encouragement I offer freely.

Villamajor de Monjardin leans back against its castled mountain. Sancho the Strong's stronghold, the town remains strong enough to hold the interest of many pilgrims. After bidding *buen camino* to a newly dear Dutchman, I continue on alone through a landscape that whispers wildness despite careful cultivation.

Civilization, Los Arcos, greets me with a dog running wild. I'm pleased and surprised to report that the cur came wagging his tail to beg for treats. Counter to experience of strays in Spain, bowser would've won a reward had I anything but chocolate, poison to pups. The parish church also pleases and surprises. Very personable, it comforts my aches, psychic or physical. Though intending to hold up here, I slam on to Sansol to make today another 40 km day, and tomorrow only 20 km, as I seek for time in Navarrette, where time once held me unwillingly.

7:30 a.m. Tues. 12/4/11

Torres del Rio, 1 km more, might have been the better target. Be vigilant for the heaven-sent shortcut shortly after. Beware of 2 km tacked onto your route past Logrono. The pleasing path sickens pilgrims once they see how far they walk for naught. Past the park, head to the highway. Don't streel around the lake. Before Logrono, the route cleaves an unpleasant industrial area. Consider alternatives. Do not miss the principal temples of Viano or Logrono though. Duty rewards, yet neither can match the parish church of little Navarrette. Pack dumped at the municipal hostel (by 4:30), I hotfooted to the golden sanctuary. In a field of gold, I plant a seed of gold from which I expect no yield.

Wed. 13/4/11

From Navarrette this New Yorker must go now, though I learned yesterday that I've already passed the clique of Californians chased since St. Jean. I left word and waited till the church doors opened again on unusual religious art (other than the glistening sanctuary). I desired to direct my compatriots to beauty, as I had many others. Besides, songs had come to mind that I knew known singers would appreciate. More importantly, one of their number had accepted a chess challenge from me before fleeing. If he fails to show today, we'll all call him chicken.

The shared meal prepared last night put me in the shitter at double-time twice. Today finds me reasonably recovered, despite my disturbed sleep and passing those who prepared the meal that poisoned me. Deliberately? Shared meals can be fun and rewarding, but too many cooks can spoil more than broth.

One Swiss hiker hounded me all the way to Najera, a town stayed in before. Had memory filed Najera properly, I might have rested there again, but today I fully intend to finish another 40 km day. "If super fit Swiss cannot catch me, who can?" I queried, only to spot a vaccarro peregrino riding into town.

Just prior to entering on shank's mare, I paused to read a large sign about a "battle between Roldan [sic] and the Syrian giant." The foremost knight of Christendom dueled for days against the undefeated titan who ruled Najera. Eventually, Roland discerned the sole weak spot of his enemy. Triumphant, this good sir also pillaged the Christian city of Pamplona, after promising the opposite. Local Basques (not Saracens) then rallied to slaughter the rear-guard of Charlemagne's Frankish army. Commanding there, Roland refused to blow the signal bugle until too late for rescue, due to the fatal flaw of pride, or maybe the fatalistic acceptance that he only reaped what he had sown.

Najera bursts with history. A Royal monastery/mausoleum dates to the middle-ages, but caves dug above tell older tales. Many stores, eateries and hostels care for modern pilgrims. My only objection turns on bringing the current camino by one more stone-milling plant. Even Don Quixote would hesitate to charge these satanic mills.

- - - - -

On the other side of the city, the equestrian rests in shade with his panting pup while allowing his fine steed to graze. Here I meet again an eccentric Englishman and hike ahead of him only with some difficulty, though he marches with his boots unlaced! Temptingly good as that might feel on swollen feet, he'll be sorry later. If "only mad dogs and Englishmen go out in the midday sun," you may say that leaves me in the role of insane canine. No, the mad dawgs bark in his boots, and will soon bite. The wool watchcap he wears will hurt him too.

A patch of shade located for lunch, I cooled my heels until the Brit caught up. The sun beats down brutally in April (October too). Any attempt to cross this pitiless plain anytime between crosses over the line into insanity.

- - - - -

Wanting to ensure a place in a special albergue, I push all the 20 km to Santo Domingo and keep ahead of all, even the Swiss fellow and the Marlboro man. To me this hostel, run by a dedicated lay order, continues the practical devotions of a medieval Santo Domingo (not to be confused with the founder of the Dominican Order). Besides saints Jim and Rocky, the local Dom comes highest in the pantheon of pilgrim pals. His cathedral presents an artistic and architectural wonder—and agricultural! This church holds the only continually occupied chicken coop I've ever seen enshrined. No voodoo temple, this cloistered place proffers peace. Isodore, a Spanish saint, patron of farmers (and my native parish), also appropriately receives requests for intercessions here. The religious order that cares for us keeps the flock too, for weekly rotation. The stranger birds, bigger birdbrains, walk with me.

The poultry represent a miraculous, funny story (of a serious sort), particularly pertinent to pilgrims. I'll not spoil the surprise by telling it. You really have to be there, to see a second miracle the first produced: an intriguing cathedral and a huge refugio, supported by an admirable community within a fine community, one embodying the Camino, as their founder envisaged centuries ago. [Not according to plan, more Moors seem to reside here than anywhere else—globalization again.]

Let me stipulate I did not complain above about the weather. Though El Camino traverses a green desert, what's pilgrimage without sweat? You and God note that I noted today's dusty path would morph into a sea of mud and suffering if today's clouds let loose.

At last we walkers (an Irishman, an Englishman and a staunch Frenchman) reached the ridge where once two angels pressed my pace and disappeared. This time a water fountain waited, the work of angels surely. After a brief break, I shoved my frayed soul on to Santo Domingo's care before 6:00 p.m. Of course the cowboy could have cantered past me at anytime, but kindness (to a young mount and an old man) restrained the reins.

Hiker's Tip: The trick to attacking hills—always strike with vigor. Lean into the incline, letting your staff catch you while punishing the slope. Allow gravity (the arms of God) and your arms to help your legs climb.

You can coast downhill if you like, but never up.

Tip for horsemen: Don't bother your ass, or horse. All water along the route must flow with all the poisonous runoff from Spain's intensive agri-business. You may end up walking in riding boots.

Hiker's Tip: Wearing double pairs of socks does work effectively against blisters, but all the Germans carry special roll-on oil. Any oil should reduce friction. The opposite, soaking in brine, might work too.

CHAPTER 7
Santo Domingo to Carrion

Hiker's Tip: Crossing the verdant desert, I employed the damp towel trick to ward off sunburn and to dry laundry.

Hiker's Tip: Localities cover much of the Camino in yellowish brick. Remember, however, more than a fake wizard waits behind the curtain in Us (not Oz).

Hiker's Tip: Light candles in the chapels passed.

Thurs. 14/4/11

From Santo Domingo at 10 a.m. Another late start! Internet and laundromat duties delayed me. This albergue provides both services. While clothes swirled, I whirled around town once more, taking care to leave undone enough to justify a future visit. Departing Santo Domingo I helped to herd sheep from a path onto the highway. (No, not for badness.) Admittedly I aided the shepherds primarily so not to vie for the path with 200 dirty sheep. More appropriately here, the trail also swings me by a poultry farm. Shades of the Appalachian Trail in Georgia! The olfactory glands spur my memory more cruelly than expected.

Setting out at 10 a.m. means no other pilgrim meets the eye, before or behind. All who find my petty game of "Pass-the-Pilgrims" puerile should know I never chase anyone who never challenged me (even inadvertently). Serious purpose does underlie my sport. Even a silly challenge can motivate tired feet. Today should require no encouragement, however, to reach a reasonable 35 km, or Villafranca Montes.

Moreover, as hiking with others runs counter to the purpose of pilgrimage, a serious seeker will need to put on speed not to lose the real game. To avoid the trap of trivial social conventions or trudging behind trudgers all day or stewing your soul in a pedestrian world, sometimes a walker must run. Only slightly less dispiriting, to spot not another soul, hour after hour, can leave your soul hungry and malnourished. Try to catch others then, to interact minimally as you pass. Finding out from where folks hail can interest greatly a man with no country, and no home.

During the first half day, I passed fifteen pilgrims, whose names I also learned, six German, two Swiss, one Belgian, one Italian, one English, one Dutch, one Dane, one Canadian, one Japanese. The second day, fifteen Spaniards outnumbered eleven Germans; eight Koreans doubled the next most numerous nation, the Dutch; French and Swedes followed with three; from the U.S.A., Canada, Brazil, England, and South Africa couples came; Denmark, Hungary, and Luxemburg sent single representatives to complete an eclectic list of fifty-seven. By the third day I began passing people already dusted once, but, not counting them, three Koreans, three Belgians, two Germans, two Spaniards, two Canadians met me.

Now the notating grows tedious, but today's crop still shows the variety that a speedy pace produces. In another sense, variety lessened on the Camino, as all who would hike 1,000 kilometers or more I call compadres, if not compatriots. We share more than we do with most folks back home. The numbers from Protestant countries does surprise, but remember that northern prods escape winter by hiking here.

Germans outnumber even Spaniards; Koreans unexpectedly beat most countries, at least in the early stages of the pilgrimage. After flying so far, "the Irish of Asia" attempt to complete the full course in order to secure indulgences. Though largely not large or unfit, they unfortunately tend not to finish, due to a clash of climate and culture. Females particularly, because feminine modesty survives in Korea, have difficulty with the lack of public facilities in a hot dry climate. They hesitate to rehydrate properly. I can't stress enough the importance of drinking liters of plain H20, daily, and avoiding caffeine and alcohol.

Failure to rehydrate leads to all sorts of injury which walkers usually fail to associate with insufficient water.

Personally, my right knee has been weakening for weeks. Ignored so far, this threat had best be heeded now. Now I know the distance remaining can be completed in time if only I take more care, employ more patience. This I do promise God to do, as I'm sure He has other things to do besides producing miracles for me every few miles.

- - - - -

Two consecutive days, yellow arrows direct pilgrims around public parks instead of through. Do locals try to annoy? Granon's misdirection disturbs most, as the entire town constitutes a diversion. Give us a break!

Good news and bad news: aggravating agricultural traffic lessens on the local dirt roads; most of what does travel is the worst—cursed sprayers fixed to ten-ton tractors. Gravel-pack roads designed for donkey carts can't withstand modern traffic. My lungs struggle with the dust, never mind the herbicide, which looks totally superfluous on these perfect fields. Agribusiness replaces rural custom, with directives.

Disappointed to arrive in Belorado too early to settle down in good conscience, I couldn't keep a promise to myself to stay in an historic albergue, a remnant of El Cid's fortress. Pressing on, I'm consoled to learn that hostel has closed down, due to wear and tear (high turnover). The refuge where I did stay last time remains open on the approach to town, where exhaustion and ice cream tempt one to stop. A lively lovely civic square merits the march into town. Before the parish church I sang Irish/Aussie songs with an Aussie, before continuing out of town after a short sit. As no one pushes me, I refuse to push myself.

Exiting town, I must comment that Belorado looks more depressed and dirty now. Maybe locals would say the same about me, but they would lie. Last time I did traverse town at sunrise, as opposed to sundown today. The periphery of town doesn't appear familiar either. What way do I go?

- - - - -

The path has surely altered entirely before Villafranca. I'm blessed to land before full darkness (9:00), and even more fortunate to locate an albergue attached to a luxury hotel, St. Anton Abad. The pilgrim menu here might make you want to give up wandering. Extremely helpful, staff treat pilgrims politely, like full-paying guests.

The small wing for pilgrims, cannot match the huge albergue of Santo Domingo, but faces no pressure to keep order with strict rules. I wouldn't want the bigger albergue run any other way, but to escape strict rigidity on the Camino refreshes. For instance, I dined in the luxury hotel till 11:00 p.m.

Fri. 15/4/11, Villafranca to Burgos

All hostels come complete with plagues of bacteria, viruses, and allergens. I woke again this morning with the makings of a cold. So far, my exertions have ever sweated out every infection along the road. Pray this trend continues all the way to Santiago. St. James help me otherwise.

The huge rapid turnover of guests aside, the lack of soap and sleep does nothing to stem contagion in cold drafty dorms, or in close musty bunkrooms. The variable weather of spring or autumn doesn't help either, but the extremes of summer and winter might wax and wane lethally. Beware dehydration. Keep taking vitamins.

Consider starting in Arles on April Fool's Day to hit St. Jean and the Pyrenees by May Day. That will nearly guarantee safe passage over the mountains, and preserve you from the hottest crossing of Castile's cruel plains. I would not want to try any later, but could plan a campaign for a fortnight earlier. If you must start in Italy too, make the border before March, the traditional martial month. Avoid Holy Week (and crop-spraying week) in Spain to miss plagues of cyclists and other fatal dangers. Doubt drinking-water at all times.

Intending to shower and breakfast by now, I've done neither. Shaving I did accomplish, as the hotel manager instructed me—during a dream—not to appear unshaven in the ritzy dining room. How's that for advanced communication and management skills? That left me no time for breakfast though.

- - - - -

All right, that does it. This time I mean it. No more larkin' about. Steady progress from now on. My faith feels a bit shaken. Faith in my own ability to will my way to

Santiago has been bludgeoned by the long uncertain trek into Burgos city center, after a beating delivered by the mountains protecting Villafranca.

Hiker's Tip: Never trudge a long urban trek during siesta. I don't know why that stretch of sidewalk pains a soul so, but everybody agrees it's deadly. Authorities made it worse by planting the municipal hostel on the far side of town.

Fortunately, four years ago a downtown parish albergue saved me miraculously. Locating it again, I found it closed until May, but (even more miraculously) the municipality had relocated its refuge downtown in a specifically redesigned and redeveloped venerable building. Though purpose-renovated, a serious design flaw (due to government regulation) spoils otherwise attractive accommodation. Though charging the least (€4), Burgos Hostel does provide soap (again miraculously). However, know I would not pay more than €4 to stay there.

- - - - -

Note, old communal wash-houses, all washed up now, remain to shade and shelter pilgrims along the way.

Sat. 16/4/11, Burgos to Castlejeritz

Burgos Albergue crams hundreds so closely together, the girl in bunk #530 now ranks as the prettiest with whom I ever slept. Call me a heel, but I don't even know her name. As just punishment, stabbing pain now needles my left heel. I take pains to stipulate that my suffering never compares with that of four years ago, when exiting Burgos. That memory also aids my endurance of Friday's endless sidewalk. My discomfort comes as a gentle reminder from God. The kind hint may not overcome the stamina-stealing of

Tuesday's dubious dinner. If Navarrette saved my first camino, it may yet kill the second.

At least I've hobbled into Horndillias by lunch, despite a late start. This village comes first among "the hidden towns" I well recall cursing and blessing on my first camino. On that trip, I tripped over the town in the dark. This time, knowing its hiding place, I readily located Horndillas in broad daylight and hoped to find a perfectly rustic experience, dining on home-cooking in a country inn. Had I arrived minutes earlier, I'd have fulfilled my quest. Instead, a long wait produced only disappointment.

Still, because the inn had run out of everything desired, I had time to "entertain the troops", hikers bivouacked in the town square between tavern and church. My comrades in the next hidden town, Hontanas, I similarly regaled with song and story. Leaving with a strawberry Magnum ice cream in one hand, a banana in the other, this *bon vivant avec bon courage* also carries: smiles and cheers received

6:30 a.m., Palm Sunday 17/4/11, Castrojeritz

I trust you're impressed with my early departure, but I am not, and soon halt to write. Arrow/shell signposts hide well enough in full daylight, as can sheep shit, not to mention food shops and shortcuts. Why walk in the dark? Until now, I've respected early risers (5:00). Now I know them for noxious fools, noisily stumbling about in the dark until dawn at 7:00. Why? We're not in August. Some hikers even wear parkas all day! As light graces the hills, a passel of pilgrims just passed an arrow unaware. No, I didn't let birdbrain early birds fly wrong, but I will still beat them to Santiago. Worms will get these early birds first.

Hiker's tip: If flying to Spain, why would you want not to see it? You can't even ascertain a day's nature in the dark before dawn, never mind find food and shelter, or info and events. I do recommend leaving this town at first light, however, in order to attain the plateau beyond in time to view an inspiring sunrise behind.

A new shelter, or viewing stand, awaits atop one of the most infamous inclines on the Camino. Relax and enjoy awhile, but before the real heat hits, continue on the long, dry descent into Boadilla del Camino (20 km). You'll make Fromista then for lunch. Dally there to delay trudging the harsh sun-drenched stretch out of town.

In point of fact, all who beat me out of bed I beat to the next town. One woman climbed the aforementioned infamous incline without employing her expensive hiking poles for more than a fashion accessory. She prattled as she progressed with her companion, never even noticing the magnificent sunrise until I pointed it out while passing.

Speaking of pains, a new one attacks my back. Having already done everything to lighten my pack, I don't know what more to do. Stretching my back along with my legs would have been a good idea. Too late! Will this jab develop into the debilitater that finally puts me off the trail? Regardless, approaching Boadilla before 11:00 a.m., I galloped to the call of the bell, into the main square, nicely in time for Mass (in case you worried about me). Oddly, the poor parish does not distribute palms, but rather sprigs of a local plant, like gorse or heather. After Mass, I repaired to the recommended albergue opposite, where more singing flowed—requests even, and not easy ones.

- - - - -

Villacezar earns a pause with its Templar "White Church." Quite unique. Having forgotten my plan to find it, I applied the whip when sudden recollection struck me. Having hiked 40 km, I arrived in time to view inside and to see outside a tour bus arrive—too late! I enjoyed both, plus the restaurant serving on the temple square.

What I've said for shade-less stretches before, goes double for the killing zone that extends from Villacezar to Carrion. Pointed straight into the setting sun, I envisaged a golden ball rolling down a bowling alley to hit a spare—me. Still, the game must be easier than at midday, and I felt capable of keeping ahead of all other hikers, even the pack-less female power-walkers who fell in behind me. Admittedly, they did gain, but I needed to stop to pray over my gimpy right knee, which had already carried me 45 km today, and from Italy recently.

I'd also planned to overnight in Villacezar, but decided to carry on to Carrion where I secured a bed in the historic hostel of the Poor Clares Convent (€5). As the price does not imply luxury, Spartan accommodation did not disappoint. A fairly elegant eatery nearby didn't either. It provided the best waiter who's ever worked a room. I told him so when leaving a tip. I even discovered at this restaurant that I don't hate beetroot. Amazing what one can learn on Camino. I considered most delicious finding the above tour group still at dinner, though they had passed me back in Villecezar.

CHAPTER 8
Carrion to O'Cebreiro (Galicia)

1 a.m., Mon. 18/4/11, "Carry on" to "Shotgun."

Slept in again. The Poor Clares must act more Christian than the Benedictines. Today I am granted opportunity to behave as kindly as one hiker can to another. To an unusual Japanese girl (I call "Freckles" for the usual reason), I could give water. Once the plateau past Castrojeritz had been passed, I gave up carrying the extra bottle of water lugged all the way from Amerikay. Drinking it myself reduced pack weight. However, fortunately for Freckles and me, while still bearing an unopened liter, I found her thirsty. Refilling the insanely small bottle she'd brought, I pledged mine to her service, while continuing to carry it. Joshing, I called her Irish too, "Roisin Dubh" (Dark Rose), but her proper name means "sunshine" and fits her nicely too.

I already call a woman from Maine that, though she quit the Camino at Carrion due to leg injury. Knowing how hardy Mainers must be, I know how serious her injury must be, though she gave no indication besides quitting. Her alarmingly contagious grin indicated only her appreciation of my musical Irish parting.

At my pace I continue meeting very many very varied pilgrims, but also manage to walk alone (with my troubled soul and bad bowels). Only cursed cyclists cannot be escaped. Down they swoop on us plodders, like harpies from hell. They might shout *"buen camino"* after shooting past in a pack. Nearly clipping your pack, they startle the shite out of you. Something really should be done. Bikes have no business on this medieval path.

- - - - -

Calzadilla de la Cuiza, yet another hidden village, I remember well and fondly. Having once found shelter there on a dark and stormy night, I forgot what a long dry trudge a pitiless sun would make of the path from Carrion. I ought to have set out earlier. Many pilgrims pass me now as I siesta in a fine hotel restaurant. That leaves me untroubled, as I should have no trouble reaching my designated destination for the day, Sahagun, before 7 p.m., and probably before all who pass. Forty kilometers today should put me in a city large enough to guarantee a bed, preferably at "the Cluny," the historic hostel missed last time. This municipality, taking its duties seriously, has converted an old monastery and provided a policeman hospitalero. I only assume he permits inmates to depart in the morning.

- - - - -

Oh again I jinx myself by noting down my plans in advance. I did hit Shotgun by 7:30 at least, but only by hard pushing. A young Spanish peregrino nearly tagged me, pressed me all the way, though I had vowed not to succumb to pressure from people today. My "opponent" held all the home ground advantages: fully acclimatized, he had local knowledge of language, customs, shortcuts, toilets, etc., and only a daypack to carry. I could only beat him by running. I vow now: no "Marine's Hymn" tomorrow. With local knowledge, I could have cut 5 km off the Camino today, which showed more twists than a snake on a barber pole.

I did beat the boy to the Cluny, but possibly only because he knew to go elsewhere in Sahagun. Amazing the difference four years can make in a hostel. From freshly remodeled and tightly run to unsafe and unsanitary, a hostel can fall sharply. For the first time, I sought a refund after one look at the dorm, and before seeking other accommodation. Ha! Fat chance! Stuck! I nearly left anyway, but better beds cost more if found.

I'm not proud of the tricks used to ensure my personal security and sound sleep. You can just avoid the place. Alternatively, you may find it all restored. Good luck.

7:00 a.m., Tues. 19/4/11, Shotgun to Villarente

Another 40 km day, and my heels bruise now as my shoe-soles have been beaten to hell. My shoes, probably never up to this task, could have cost me much more, and still spared me no pain. Though confident in wearing this pair home, I'll take it easy on them today anyway. Yesterday's race would never have happened had I not stopped to play good Samaritan. Attempting to provide more water to Freckles, I waited pointlessly as she never came, and competition did. At least the contest carried me past the halfway point to Santiago: Templarios (from St. Jean). Of course, you can't trust Templar promises, and I must continue past Santiago to Finisterre too.

- - - - -

Whatever agribusiness sprays in Spain, it doesn't affect the very varied birdlife. From magnificently gliding storks to petite sweet-singing wrens, the early pilgrim gets quite a show, whatever the early bird gets.

Speaking of singing, I've been repeating to myself "The Battle Hymn of the Republic" for days. What did a farmer, who crossed the road in front of me, telepathically whistle from his barn? You guessed it. In Spain!?

- - - - -

Nope, the way runs way weirder than even I thought. Whistling came not from the farmer, but from one who lay in wait for me. The devil who challenged me yesterday just fell in behind. Well, I am having none of it. Having to pee anyway, I departed the path. He stopped to say so, he so wanted to race. Even if interested, I can't humor him today. I have my own agenda and memories to revisit. What scares me, only God and Satan knew my plan to take the old route. I reiterate that Satan rules this route. Enough on the demonic however, I come this way in daylight to find an angel who rescued my first Camino. In Calzadilla (yet another one), in a little restaurant, she fights the forces of darkness. This Calzadilla manages to hide on a hill! Yet, no devil dares cross an angel's threshold (first on the right).

A meal so nice I ordered it twice, the proprietress refused to repeat, insisting instead on treating me to a better, different dish requested first. Even more delicious for me, she serves up my message, penned in her guest book four years before: "To an angel of God's mercy."

- - - - -

Maybe no hell-dog hounded me this trip, but the first rain in Spain nipped at me on my way to Calzadilla.

- - - - -

No sooner does a lone weary figure decry aloud the absence of any rest area on the Wicked Way than a new purpose-built lean-to appears. This explains why one hikes in the spring following a holy year. The Camino remains ready for the crowds of pilgrims who no longer crowd the trail and hostels. Not so many flies buzz as in the fall. On these many miles past Calzadilla, I might be the only soul on Earth.

- - - - -

Leaving town without taking on more water looks more and more like serious misjudgment. In my long dry search, I suddenly feared water finding me. Massive storm clouds roiled and rolled over the horizon. A visible downpour to my left joined sheets of gray swooping from my right. Still no sign of shelter for me. I did pass up an open garden shed, despite fear mounting, dark as the massing clouds overhead.

At this point did I cry out to God to help me, promising to recognize as miraculous any shelter He might produce on that featureless plain. That's when the ground opened to swallow me. Sure, 'twould have done the same for any passing pagan, but the earth opened for this pilgrim on request, between Villamarco and Reliegos. I call that a miracle. Thank you, Jesus, for keeping me dry.

More miracles? Mansilla de la Mulas to Villarente (6 km) I completed in forty minutes, in time to find the albergue, San Pedros, before 10 p.m. Unfortunately, as the only sign hangs unlit, I passed it in the dark, but managed to come-about to find one of the best hostels on El Camino. Pity, I've no time to fully appreciate the facilities. From 1 p.m. to 10 p.m., no sight of hikers met my eye until this albergue. Nice to be home now.

8:00 a.m. Wed. 20/4/11, From Villarente

I honestly do not know at what distance to aim today. Leon at least must be reached early as I have errands to run in a big city. This city comes well supplied with historic hostels. Should I push on regardless, despite the long days of many miles, not to mention the heavy rain falling now? The worst of the latter we'll wait out anyway. The café near San Pedros Hostel (El Horno) makes an exceptionally pleasant waiting room.

My gamble paid off as the downpour did ease up within the hour, though rain looks likely to fall all day.

Loping into Leon with little difficulty, I may run into trouble with the stupid siesta. You locate me in an unaffected café, enjoying a perfect tortilla potatas with tapas and freshly squeezed OJ. Credit must go to my borrowed guidebook for my easy entry into this city. Hard rain and soft mud presented no obstacle because the book suggested taking the bus (to avoid poor scenery). No, I did not board a bus, but the wimpy suggestion so outraged this peregrino, I fairly steamed into town.

Opting for the bus, the guidebook opines, is perfectly acceptable because everyone's camino differs and cannot be judged by another's standards. Presumably fibbing about completing the route is also OK, as truth is relative. The author further suggests sparing a prayer on the bus for the poor benighted blighters trudging beside the highway when you sweep by. This pseudo Buddhist crap made me mad enough for emotion to move me over the hump into Leon. Even in the rain and mire, the ease with which I finished pleased me. Credit really belongs to the locals, who do distance the Way from the highway, contrary to the libelous Buddhist's book. No way the walk compares to Burgos.

Even the bad entry to Burgos can easily be improved by simply not stumbling in during siesta.

I have only one word for my readers. Two words would nicely sum up my opinion of the pinhead penning the Zen shite. (OK—not nicely.) My one-word advice, "Walk!" always applies when on a Christian pilgrimage. Christians believe in God, in right and wrong. If you promise Christ, who undertook a harder hike for you, that you will walk to Santiago for Him and for your intentions (not to mention fellow pilgrims), you can't just jump aboard a bus anytime you please or when the view fails to please. That possibility cannot even occupy your mind if you claim the title "peregrino." If you call yourself a pilgrim and take the route, good-will or bed belonging to pilgrims, *walk*! If that hurts, that's good. Were the way easy, why would we vow to walk it? If in pain, sing for joy!

Even if you can't carry a tune, a tune can carry you, until flesh pulls from bone. When you really can't take another step, call out to God for a miracle. God does do miracles. If no miracle comes, before boarding a bus confess to God and man that you failed, but will try again (God willing). Even if you don't believe in God, have some belief in yourself—for God's sake! I don't advocate masochism. *Au contraire*, the duty of any pilgrim pushes him to rack only his brain, for means to ease his journey, the better to complete his vow and beat the devil.

Whatever truth and honor allow, they do require. I don't advise, for instance, galloping under pack across the country, like one fool sinner now springing to mind. Let me mention though, for two days I have kept my pledge to resist Marine Hymn sprints. Forty km per day I cover anyway, despite daily downpours. I considered hiking farther today, until the Almighty unleashed the worst drenching of the day, directly outside the Villadangos hostel (an old schoolhouse). With only an hour of watery light left, and no guaranteed bed ahead, I felt best stopping at 40.

Before bed, I'm duty bound to credit another Spaniard for spurring me along today. To a man, Spanish walkers hike doggedly. In one more slap at the guidebook, I point out that exiting Leon hits harder than entering. One section descends into a hellish mess altogether, especially after a heavy rain. Keep on truckin'.

Holy Thursday, 9:00 a.m. 21/4/11, Villadangos to El Ganso?

Late start today. I woke lightheaded and heavy-handed, presumably due to dehydration. Pack repairs press on me. I must take care now, as having passed Leon (El Camino's great divide), I can smell the Santiago cake. Having come all the way from Italy, I can almost taste that almond tarte. The illusion endangers me as a few hundred kilometers ain't nothing to sneeze at. At least I haven't got a cold. Walking myself into exhaustion in the rain, and sleeping in overcrowded drafty old schoolhouses (in three-tier bunks), after sharing showers and toilets with other folk abusing their health, I really should feel sicker. Hope I didn't just jinx myself.

At least I remain rational, not delirious, though my vision does seem blurred.

Oddly, the greatest danger of dehydration comes on cold, wet walks. Beware sunburn on cloudy days too.

Maybe on Holy Thursday I'll catch one of Spain's famous liturgical processions. Trying to witness a rain-delayed one on Not-So-Bad Tuesday resulted in my needing to run to the next town, Villarente, in the dark. Let's see if we're luckier today. Someday I'd like to stay where the Knights of St. John held sway, Hospital de Orbigo.

Incidentally, the obvious analogy of my beginning the Camino in the fall as an agnostic, only to return in the spring as a resurrected gnostic, happens totally coincidently. We walk now where I recall treading on hard frost in October and feeling trod upon. Those autumn days always warmed to hotter than now though. Wish I'd written my French Foreign Legion song to help me along then. In Orbigo, Hospitalers once jousted Templars to martial music.

From Orbigo to Astorgas

15 kilometers lays down harder demands than appearances suggest, especially the final few. You might ignore the arrow that directs you off the main thoroughfare into town. You'd avoid a monster construction, more obstructive than constructive. Three hours took me the long way to Astorgas, and the town held me for three. An excellent albergue offered free Internet and toilet. Opposite, an ancient chapel provided Mass on a holy day of obligation, plus a presentation of the processional tableaux carried tomorrow, as did a "rival" church down the street. The cathedral reigns over all, assisted by Gaudi-designed Bishop's Palace Museum.

Parks and squares are stunningly set to offer great views, particularly for testing my hypothesis: that Astorga females look better than the average senorita in northern Spain. Confirmation looks likely but requires more study.

- - - - -

Leaving Astorgas took longer than expected (as you might have expected), but still left enough time to reach El Ganso theoretically, especially as my legs did not limp down the hill like last time. However, recalling how desperately I searched for shelter four years ago in the dark, not to mention the night before last, I decide to settle for one village short of the mark: Sante Catalina. It sounds (and is) better than El Ganso. Enough already of running in the rain, I'm stopping here. After 9 p.m., darkness falls too, but light lasts much longer than in the fall. Yet, I have hiked solo from Astorgas. Not a soul in sight.

Good Friday, 9:00 a.m. 22/4/11, From Ste. Catalina

The great Templar Castle of Pontferrada stands 43 km away, my destination for today, unless I listen to the guidebook waffle about depression. I hold in my hand the cure: a pilgrim's staff. If action fails to cure any depression in your head, come closer; I'll cure you with my staff, by making a depression in your head.

I'd like to use my stick on the fellows who follow me to shout from the bushes, "Cuckoo," all along the Camino. Come out and call me that to my face! I'll bash out your birdbrain! Though not questioning the truth of the derogatory comment, I won't stand for anonymous insults. (I jest.)

St. Jim kindly stopped me in Ste.Catalina as I see no sign of El Ganso's albergue—even in broad daylight.

Never try too hard to repeat a treat. Next time, I'll try to reach before dark Rabanal del Camino instead. It looks to suit a tired, hungry pilgrim. A cute mini-monastery offers free accommodation and board, plus a taste of monastic life. You'll need all the nourishment, rest and prayer you can get for the trail beyond Rabanal.

In wet weather the climb to the legendary Cross of Iron grows abominable. Truly, no path exists for much of the distance. Next time, from the outset I'll take the road, nearly to Acebo (first town on the far side of the pass).

When you reach the Cross of Iron, Peregrino, be ready to recognize it with your own ritual, as the symbol of your salvation. You'll see a million souls did before you. **WARNING:** That will include the bus-takers.

Have your camera ready when you reach Acebo as crossing the peaks will mean a new (very old) style of architecture greets you. The new style extends down to Molinaseca in a verdant vale, where coachloads of tourists can view the quaintness. To reach there from above, the pilgrim must follow another wretchedly rough and overgrown trail. In the springing of the year, however, this path promises to grow well worth the trouble, as long as the rain stops and no ticks lurk in the bushes. Sheer cliff walls and rock outposts protect a treasure of wild ferns and flowers wondrous to all the senses. Birds and brooks delight better only the ears.

All in all, today's camino untypically reminds me of the Appalachian Trail, in good and bad ways. Fortuitously, the route onward from Molinaseca to Pontferrada provides several kilometers of sidewalk through empty countryside. That pavement appeared as an answer to prayer, as I never departed Molinaseca until after Good Friday services, which left me little time before dark and locked hostels.

Thanks to my Mex/Oz pal from '07, the location of the principal hostel in Pontferrada nicely came to mind. Gracias, Jose. There I last saw you, as I hobbled onward despite the late hour. Incidentally, I did remember to thank God for today's rain, as it could easily have snowed instead on a mountaintop in this season, as nearby peaks testified (or threatened). Let me also express gratitude to a new friend, Gos (Jos), Flemish for Joseph coincidently. A totally different character from Jose, he might fairly be called Phlegmish. We developed a rapport regardless, as Gos speaks English, but also because we seem to move at similar speed towards Santiago. Though slower, he is steadier, and usually already in the albergues when I arrive to sleep. A plodding Prod, he yet shares my serious view of pilgrimage and frowns on cycling clubs and day-trippers claiming peregrino status in our hostels.

Lastly, I should thank the Templars for their traditions of resistance to Saracens and hospitality to pilgrims. These traditions built the castle and cathedral towering above me, and also the peaceful passage underfoot. This area remains blessed with order and prosperity due to bold efforts by the Templars long ago. However, much as I'd like to be gracious, I cannot. Beware the Templars. They sell security for liberty and heresy for truth.

Holy Saturday, 8:15 a.m. 23/4/11, Pontferrada to Vega de Valcarce

My early start already ruined by my returning for these very notes (left under a pillow with my pen and penlight), Pontferrada detained me too, even at that early hour, with many historic places. Afterwards, that secure fortress town yet required a great effort to escape. We'll see 11 a.m. before we exit, with 40 km remaining to do today. These feet better pass folks big-time this day. Having forsworn the Marines Hymn, I resort to the Battle Hymn. Verse 3 spurs best:

> He has sounded forth the trumpet that shall
> never call retreat.
> He is sifting out the hearts of men before
> the judgment seat.
> Be swift my soul to answer him, be jubilant my feet!
> Our God is marching on!

Something you probably don't know, Julia Howe (the author) had married a Dr. Howe, one of John Brown's "secret six" sponsors. By supplanting "John Brown's Body," Julia surmounts Brown and her husband in history.

- - - - -

More than a dozen pilgrims I passed in about two hours, the latest two a nice Irish couple on the final stage of a three-year camino. They seem to like my songs and certainly enjoy this Templar route. Two more hours brings the total to twenty dusted, and me to Villafranca del Bierzo, right to the same restaurant where four years ago Koreans (total strangers to me) toasted me as the famous "Fast Michael." Today, a perfectly sunny day allows me to sit outside at the tables on the square, but I prefer inside, having suffered no shortage of sunlight. As soon as I finish my paella Valencia, I'll order El Burger Americano before moving outside to join café society.

- - - - -

Well, two hours in Villafranca, and a full belly, should have granted all other peregrinos sufficient head start. If I only passed another four, that was not due to my going slower. Afternoon only yielded four, though I still walked another 40 km day. Learned today, I must confess, at least two alterations in the Camino were made only in my faulty memory, as towns possess very similar names and appearances.

Easter 24/4/11, 8:30 a.m., From Vega de Valcarce, only to O'Cebreiro

Hey, I fancy the Irish sounding name, all right? Besides, O'Cebreiro hostel supposedly possesses the best facilities anywhere near here. Most importantly, I trust the village will have an Easter Mass near noon, and perhaps a procession. However, Spaniards wouldn't dare darken Easter with black shrouded figures groaning under brutal tableaux. (I'd thought myself raised in the old, dark religion!)

See how kind God treats me now? Though departing Vega an hour later than hoped, I left with great heart in search of the risen Lord. A little desperately, but in good faith, I stretched my stride, having already brushed by Vega's not very venerable church, the ugliest in Spain. Besides, at that hour, the necessary wait would be weighty on one already pressed for time. The O'Cebreiro goal had been picked for a half-recalled chapel and hostel, but only after going some distance did I fully recall the difficulty of the task given myself. Unless memory fails again, the trail will traverse a high mountain to the final province, Galicia. No wonder now the Gaelic "O" in O'Cebreiro.

- - - - -

My success seems the more miraculous as:

1) Though the devil dragged like deadweight on my backpack, this Irish boy attacked the incline, with all the power God gave him, renewed at the thought of Galicia waiting.
2) Even if no Mass waited, a personal resurrection in Galicia on Easter Morn felt fitting and certain.
3) Clambering by five hikers climbing long before me, I paused for naught until setting foot on the older Old Sod.
4) There I snapped a signpost (with my camera, Silly), but could photo nothing more as icy mist blew down on me.
5) Though the breeze bit, I did not bid God to bother about it, because it bore no snow, as yet. Prudence pushed me onward, but I refused to bypass O'Cebreiro's Franciscan monastic chapel (oldest church on the Camino Francais).

6) Aside from the inspiring views, inside and outside the church, an excellent hostel waited with all facilities needed.

7) I did not even pause to snap the prior village, scene of the sheep stampede that nearly ended my previous camino.

8) Now, no sheep or ornery shepherd was spotted along the path into town, but an ATV suddenly roared up behind me, its black-helmeted rider looking like an anonymous assassin. Spurred, I bolted uphill to safety.

9) Spared, I attained O'Cebreiro, ahead of even cyclists, even those in cars! All want photographed with a famously fleet footer. Few possess the strength of mind to maintain my pace, even when holding the strength of limb.

10) I remembered to give credit to God for my beating the devil and reaching the church with an hour to spare. High Mass the monks sing at high noon. Hallelujah!

Having lit a big candle before our Blessed Mother for my mother, I settled in to enjoy the service, but found it marred (as would have Mother) by the lack of uniformity in the "universal" church. Even at the consecration no Continental congregation can concur on standing, sitting or kneeling. OK, we don't all need to pray in Latin, but can't we agree on any point of unanimity? Indecisive, haphazard, sloppy practice does not inspire me, and does doubtlessly not impress God. Let us not quibble about God however. This much I know: humbly I asked Him to help me up that mountain in time for Mass if it was important to Him. I did make it, miraculously appropriately.

- - - - -

Returning to disunity, I find remarkable the difference one mountain makes in architectural style. The latest proof of this truth remind me of the ancient stone structures of

Ireland, roofed in slate or thatch. Also reminiscent of Ireland, every sign posted, over most of northern Spain, will have one or two letters angrily sprayed over. Personally, I don't feel one letter worthy of confrontation and conflict, never mind killing anyone.

I, for one, am at peace with the whole world, as I go nowhere today, and just enjoyed a daytime nap after a three-course lunch. Such decadence! I expect to push myself harder for it tomorrow. For now I feel blessed to reach in 1 piece the final province of my quest, the most Irish in Spain, Galicia. In more ways than one, "I'm almost home."

Moreover, this albergue strikes me as one of the best built, best run on the Camino. Hence my feeling guilty for four years for having stiffed them €5, though that was their fault. They lacked change, and I forgot to get it in the morn. Weren't today's managers mighty amazed and amused when I paid double. They did not understand; I had to insist. **Note:** shower and laundry rooms do leave a little to be desired. I nearly left without using either.

I did make sure to eat and sing in the restaurant Venta Celta (Celtic Wind), same as last time. I commend the menu, especially the honey on local crumbly cheese, though it produces Celtic wind. Don't eat the Santiago cake. Sure it's fine, but you're not in Santiago yet. No cheating.

Galicia shares superstitions with Ireland too. I pen this page in the kitchen where two witches once brewed chestnuts for me, and witch dolls decorate everywhere. One magpie spied alone today might have scared me, was I not a lone magpie myself nowadays. Mysticism travels easily through any land this shrouded in moving mist.

Walking just a few feet from friends can put you magically into another world of solitary mystery.

CHAPTER 9
O'Cebreiro to Santiago

7:55 a.m., Mon. 25/4/11

O'Cebreiro to where-o-where? Mist misdirected me this morning, but I refound the way, though this handsome day stayed hooded until noon, typically in this mountainous province. As most of the trail now runs downhill for miles, I make fine time, when I don't stop to write, or to chat with other Irish folks. I may just go all the way to the 100 km marker, though discretion applies the brakes already.

Now that the distance diminishes to doable in days, I meet more Irish folks. Genuine Irish all right, they're less than genuine with me. Though I accepted them all as met, I find they're only nice to my face. Like AA says, the first step to fixing any problem is recognizing you have one. If our national character "goes for the cure," we'll need to quit more than drink. We certainly can fault British misrule for our flaws, but the time to get over that is over. Irishmen could be honest and sober and yet enjoy life, and be enjoyable.

I also pass one Fernando of Mexico, with whom I enjoyed discussing radical politics and the folly of Prohibition, i.e., America's War on Drugs, destructive of us and our neighbors. I won't write more on that, as I could go on all day and prefer to keep up with Fernando. A pretty, friendly, kindly Danish girl, with German hiking companion, also threatens my rep for speed. Hikers dusted a mile back require only a paragraph to catch up. Still I stop to note for the record, having cleared the last hump into Galicia—with no snow! Only now dare I to write that down. Thank you, God.

- - - - -

Holding my worn frame in check proved difficult before; now, with every half klick measured and markered, I gobble up those mightily anticipated stone markers, like M&M's. Yet, I do pause to pile rocks on an unknown person's prayer pile and stop to steady stepping stones in a stream behind me.

Be prepared to be "held up" in local bars. They might charge €1.50 for a liter of water, for instance, one costing twenty cents in a shop. Do bar owners really need that markup on a non-perishable item essential to pilgrims? I refuse to pay more than one euro in markup.

Beware the killer stairs at the 111.5 km marker in Sarria. At the foot of these, someone sagely placed an albergue, but I'm not wise enough to stop. A euro store and Internet service entice me too, but I take to the stairs. Having passed the city of Sarria, I am also confident enough to risk more jinxing—by commenting on dogs.

We just traversed the provincial border territory without a single alarum. By a certain old barn and older church nearby I have glided smoothly by, unmolested, where devil dogs once made me jump for my life. I booted through a vale of canines, but only spotted one loose Alsatian, who did not even bother to bark. Even the fairy glen, guarded by a mythically monstrous beast, my tread threaded without drawing the dread demi-god dog. Finally, I tiptoed past where "Mutt and Ruff" once performed their routine for me. No show today. Opposite another farmyard, giving wide berth to one Alsatian meant nearly stepping on another lounging in the roadside ditch. Not even a growl given, what gives? The docility of dogs begins to unsettle me. Have I stumbled into Bizarro World?

Maybe it's a miracle. Back in Montpelier I reproached St. Roch for allowing the creature that rescued him to hound me. The experience in '07 could scarcely contrast more clearly. Though big breeds still wander lose, they never bark or bite. With wagging tails, they sometimes welcome wanderers. Hark, hark! The dogs don't bark! They beg treats from a beggar. You'd swear St. Roch precedes me with a tranquilizer gun. I'm certainly stunned.

Subdued dogs may be due to last year's holy year, another reason to hike in the subsequent season. Last year's crowds left the dogs all barked out. Some brutes actually broke their voice boxes, while others merely grew bored. Ones driven mad, or who drove their owners mad, were probably put down. Owners possibly grew tired of warnings from the authorities (civil or cleric) to curb their critters. A couple of the latter must have bitten pilgrims and, in turn, their owners (on the ass, or wallet pocket). Fines, civil suits, and destroying animals might cause considerable pain, perhaps even commiserate with the hurt inflicted by careless dog-owners.

8:15 a.m. Tues. 26/4/11, Ferreiros

Bopping by the 100 km marker meant in reality covering 58 km in one day, and reaching a bed too late really. I managed quite handily regardless but deserved gentle chiding this morning for disturbing others by arriving late. As I resolved to act more considerately, God sent an angel out-of-nowhere to warn me of a wrong turn taken.

Were the stone markers as accurate as the guidebook, I would have refused to reach 58 km and a full hostel! However, a free bed did wait 150 meters beyond, just beyond closing time, but still not beyond a big meal for a small price, though well beyond when I ought to eat before bed.

Doing 58 km also means catching up with another duly impressed cyclist, Luciano from Brazil. He calls me "Lightning Friend." New hikers I now meet daily.

Before leaving this locality, I warn all who would conduct elaborate ceremony at the 100 km marker, "Don't."

Even tokens with carefully crafted messages (to God or man) get swept daily off the concrete plinth. Before placing a rosy quartz, I broke off a piece for someone rosy, despite a life looking less than rosy. Perhaps my magic rock will stay longer if I bring away a stone discarded, to advance its supplication another kilometer closer to Santiago, and better display its message.

- - - - -

I stride determinedly slower today, but still allow no one to pass, and pass anyone sighted. I try though to avoid hiking duels. Portomarin still hit with time to spare, I enjoy the striking town. All who care to hike on may do so. If I don't catch you today, I will see you before Santiago. Few who pass now started in St. Jean even.

In my collection of churches, Portomarin's edifice figures among my favorites. Above the town, Knights of St. John raised an H.Q. fortress church, unusual even in Spain. The massive block of masonry reminds me of a church seen on the frontier of Croatia. Portomarin's recent history renders this church more special, for it fought the modern world and won. When a dam in the 1960s condemned the town, citizen parishioners moved the church (and much more), stone by stone, to the top of the hill. A high bridge, mocking the Roman bridge below, crosses the entire valley to make a dramatic entrance into town, which now looks ever to have graced that hilltop.

- - - - -

Sure enough I did jinx myself, by writing about dogs. An incident occurred today involving three stray Alsatians. Ducking into a snack bar to avoid their snarling, I was bit by a plain croissant, €1.50. I go back out now. Anything trying to bite had better like the taste of hickory wood.

- - - - -

Throngs of bus-taking, day-hiking pseudo peregrinos join El Camino after Sarria, after the last climb in the final province. They fill hostels early, leaving long-distance men to hike farther. Real pilgrims are told to accept the latecomers as true compadres, as Christ instructs us to accept the late vineyard workers. Well, I don't recall Christ welcoming phonies, hypocrites, or lukewarm liars. The Catholic Church ought not to encourage them either. Don't claim or grant the title of pilgrim unless at least a provincial border has been crossed. If you're crippled (physically or spiritually), crossing the cathedral square in Santiago should suffice between you and God, but keep that deal between you two. While at it, I'll present the case against cyclists.

Understand, I never met a cyclist I did not like, and several I met several times, despite their advantages. I admire their battle against the infernal combustion engine, but they remain unaware of damage they themselves do. Yet, since they don't want to do El Camino traditionally anyway, let cyclists remain on roads where they belong.

1) How can cyclists carry on, or reenact medieval pilgrimage, mounted in spandex on 10-speed mountain bikes?
2) Cycling clubs on the Camino do nothing different than they might on any weekend anywhere in Europe, except
3) They enjoy cheaper accommodation, at the expense of genuine pilgrims whose mystique they exploit, and except
4) They terrorize more pedestrians than they possibly could elsewhere legally. Public nuisances should face charges.
5) Like blisters and bedbugs, cyclists form an anti-pilgrim force, but a willful one.
6) They're destructive of the path itself, as their wheels form ruts; ruts become rivulets that puddle into ponds from which torrents flow to turn trails into gullies.
7) They take the beds of weary backpackers who tread the trail traditionally while cyclists coast along, and could easily peddle to the next hostel in five minutes.
8) Energy saved, cyclists tend to expend in partying, depriving real pilgrims of essential sleep.
9) Cyclists are generally accompanied by an SUV carrying provisions, packs, and parts, plus cyclists often.
10) 100 km, one day's spin on a racing bike, should hardly entitle you to the same claim as three days on foot, also paltry.

Leave footpaths to feet. Still call cyclists peregrinos, as long as they triple whatever distance backpackers must do.

Before you consider me harsh with pseudo peregrinos, consider the punishment planned for all who misuse yellow arrows directing pilgrims along the way. For all employing Camino symbols to exploit pilgrims, let the punishment be fitting and proper. After pilgrim staffs beat them black and blue, stretch their bodies beside the route (where bruises will yellow) to point the way to Santiago.

Yeah, I know, but Jesus used a whip on people who exploited faith. I'm good with being good to myself, not punishing my poor body too badly. Besides taking an extra hour for lunch in Portomarin, I took another hour from the heat of the day to rest in the first bar past the 80km-to-go mark. That leaves me another 20 km to do today, and, as we've passed 4:30 p.m., I really must go.

- - - - -

My pilgrim status (and dearth of small change) just garnered a free loaf from a bakery outside Palais de Rei.

Wed. 27/4/11,
From nowhere to somewhere near Santiago

I don't intend to belittle the very nice hostel, Casanova a Mato, that sheltered me last night. The hostel turned out particularly nice by not turning me away as had the previous two. See what I mean now? Bus riders push someone walking from Italy out into gathering gloom to do more miles before a curfew cuts him off. Around tables where pilgrims should consume meager rations carried there or ordered from the peregrino menu, cheapo partiers play at pilgrimage, at the expense of pilgrims.

The greatest price to pilgrims depletes their reputation. Property owners sold a romantic notion of hardy souls trekking on sacred quest across a continent, instead receive a pack of fakers who defecate in the shrubbery. People whose property peregrinos despoil have a right to expect some modicum of commitment from those who "trespass against them." So too do those with whom the pikers supposedly share the suffering of pilgrimage. One might suppose that God Almighty deserves a little respect, even if you don't believe in Him. God not existing only elevates man, so show more respect towards your-self. Walk the talk, that's all I'm asking.

Accuse me of unchristian feelings if you like, because I accuse pikers and fakers of the same. What does your harsh opinion make of you then? Surely nobody whose opinion I should value. Wait and see if Christ does.

I would like here to pay my respects to one phony pil-grim, an Irish woman, in the last town before Santiago. A true Christian, she insisted on giving me €5.00 for food, just because I look like I need fed. I could've taken offense but recognized she meant to honor my pilgrimage and acknowl-edge her deficiency. To her I simply say, "*Dia duit.*"

6:55 a.m., Thurs. 28/4/11, From Arca O Pines to Santiago de Compostela

Nearly busted my toes on the final leg of my journey—with my own stick! Accidents happen in predawn dorms. A teach-able moment from a heavenly Father did not hurt me.

All the German pilgers protect their feet at this hour, not from falling hickory limbs, but from blisters. They carry roll-on oil that prevents blisters by reducing friction. Presumably contains topical anti-pain and anti-bacterial substances, or any veggie oil would do as well. Only the Germans seem to have the stuff, which I've never seen advertised in Ireland or America. The F.D.A. has probably not decided yet to whom to give the profits.

- - - - -

I'm off and running now towards Santiago. No doubt I'll be passed today, as day-hikers march in legions, and the final goal rests too close. When my stride suddenly shortened behind six long-legged blondes in short shorts, I nearly stopped passing people. I fear I felt afraid to pass these girls, as they looked frighteningly fit, quite capable of walking me into the ground if challenged. Coming abreast, I sang, joked and jogged my way by, and found them as clever as cute, and also as kind, as this sorority surely allowed an old man to outstrip them. This aging pilgrim pushes past all, only partly due to all who push him. Mostly, he intends to reach the cathedral in Santiago precisely three weeks to the hour after exiting the Pilgrim Gate in St. Jean.

(P.S.: Meeting these lassies twice more today is due to destiny, not design. To them I gladly gave Santiago cake.)

- - - - -

The final stage of my journey I expect to handle easily, except for the spoiling of my perfect record: zero pilgrims passing me; me passing all. Failure looks inevitable as I'll encounter hundreds on The Way today, and my pace has begun to attract unwanted attention, celebrity even, not to mention envy and resentment. What would you have me do? Walk behind the slowest clods, and never reach my goal? I ever try to share experience and spirit with each pilgrim passed, but cheerful attempts to advise and entertain can stir ill-will. I refuse to pander to the petulant. Hell, I am an old man, well past his prime, who credits the Almighty for any power given. Ought I not use the gift?

Yesterday I paused to encourage a busload of young Germans resting by the road. Demonstrating how singing the right song can energize, I sprang away, over the next hill. I erred then, by halting shortly to pen this page. The vanguard of the Germans spied me sitting and determined to prove something to the girls in their group. Climbing the next hill, I heard three boys snicker behind me as they launched their sprint. Alerted, my own legs burst into a real demonstration of uphill running underpack—not quite the show the Aryan Youth had in mind.

Later, folks gave the impression of waiting along the way to waylay me, to test my pace in relays. Mobile phones can spoil pilgrimage in many ways. Even if no one seeks me today, surely sheer numbers should produce superior hikers. The end of the line will produce opportunity for inferior hikers to jump the city line just before me.

- - - - -

Miraculously not. Fifty folks milled about the park at the edge of town, but I cut through to the "finish line" in front of any, before or behind. More surprisingly, this magic show encored in the busy streets taken to Cathedral Square, though I never raced through the crowded thoroughfares. Opening the side door of my great sacred goal—with thirty-five minutes to spare—I saluted St. James and Jesus, who apparently appreciate perfection.

Speaking of perfection, I should also credit the successful completion of my Camino to Magnum ice cream bars. Helping me all the way from Italy. Nothing better for a non-stop breakfast, a Magnum graced my final day.

What do I notice first inside the door? Large floral sprays tastefully obscure the victims of "the moorslayer." Very P.C. Next all the duties (private and public) of a pilgrim absorb my attention, until the most important one begins: the High Mass at high noon for pilgrims. Yes, afterwards, the giant incense burner, like a potbelly stove suspended from the ceiling, did indeed swoosh and swoop the width of the nave, requiring eight men to swing it. If my ma was here, she'd surely say, "Someone's going to get hurt" or "From fun comes pain."

However, the spectacle was marred only by the unedifying sight of "pilgrims" scrambling to snap "the show," and by raucous applause—not a very proper close for solemn sacred ceremony. Besides, people sitting beside me would definitely have preferred the show to precede Mass, as the sweet smell of success off me stank more than flop sweat.

In the huge square fronting the cathedral, I faced the final danger of all pilgrimage: depression inevitably follows the elation of reaching a great goal. By good fortune, and my better efforts, sufficient time remains this trip for marching on to Finisterre. Over a millennium, pilgrims have worked out how best to counter the anticlimax. Moreover, I still possess all the songs that carried me over testing mountains and trying plains. To honor my pilgrimage, St. Patrick and St. James, plus my pledge to fellow pilgrims, I share with the square my repertoire, along with Santiago cake. I had to wait anyway for the free dinner granted pilgrims by the luxury hotel on the left of the plaza (when facing the duomo). This parador, one-time royal refugio, must by legal charter provide thirty free meals daily (ten breakfasts, ten lunches, ten dinners) to properly accredited pilgrims who queue at their garage door. That experience unsettles as much as it satisfies, and the best of the free treat is the incidental tour of the historic hotel.

Accrediting requires you to appear in the camino office off the plaza at the right rear of the cathedral. Bring your properly stamped pilgrim passport (*credentiale*) to prove your status, and be prepared for questioning. If satisfied, your inquisitors will grant you a certificate (*compostela*), all in Latin. Don't worry, the church keeps its requirements so lax (one weekend stroll suffices), those who show enough gumption to cheat deserve accrediting.

Still, your *compostela* also earns a bargain at another luxury hotel, the perfectly located Major Seminary (on the cathedral's left-rear square). Only the attic remains the haunt of seminarians or, during holidays, pilgrims. The private spartan cells of senior seminarians represents luxury to peregrinos used to crowded dorms. If the price (€23) quadruples usual accommodation cost, it quarters typical prices in town and includes the same breakfast buffet served the rich guests in this four-star establishment. By deliberately arriving mid-week, I improved my chances immensely for my privileged pilgrim experience, though arriving unaware of the possibility.

All arrangements made, I knew I ought to have felt blessed, but did not, due to the creeping depression all who complete the Camino feel. My psyche was saved only by the providential appearance of my latest Australian acquaintance and his Austrian girlfriend. Met at Casanova, entertained en route (and passed), they, I knew, would appreciate my Aussie/Irish songs. Two songs, and two pieces of Santiago tarte, did delight them, but they found most delicious my keeping a bold pledge to compadres. I also helped them find the fine accommodation mentioned.

CHAPTER 10
Santiago to Muxia, Spain, and Back Again

3:00 p.m., Fri. 29/4/11, Santiago toward Finisterre

You see me seated in a secret garden, quite extraordinarily hidden in the heart of the city. No peregrino but me, zero tourists, traverse this wild wide-open expanse in the shadow of Santiago's spires. Slightly surreally, like a dream, this untamed space presents a nightmare to hay fever sufferers but relaxes me. I'll suffer real terrors tonight though, if I don't get out of town before the spires' shadows grow any longer.

- - - - -

Past Santiago, traditional corncribs alter again, making them less worthy as national symbols surely. Nevertheless, bus shelters and mausoleums mimic corncribs. I prefer Ireland's harp to any agricultural architecture.

Again I commend Spring for pilgrimage when a zillion blossoms bloom to perfume the air. Happy I am, though, to have come to El Camino first in the fall, when all lay dormant as my soul. That makes me appreciate the Way way more now. Avoid walking through Spain in Holy Week if possible however. The entire nation celebrate's Christ's passion. If a pilgrim under time pressure, however, the only traditional procession you'll likely spy is a parade of cyclists whizzing by your ears to beat you to the hostels.

If you really desire to be alone, like Greta Garbo and me, try trekking out from Santiago towards Finisterre on any Friday afternoon but one. Ain't nobody out here, ahead or behind. I studiously strive to take this stroll through the woods nice and easy. To properly enjoy this dander, you may need to like eucalyptus. Though these tall invaders aren't my favorite, I do appreciate this shaded wind-down after the adrenaline rush of the race into Santiago. That city provides additional buzz as the destination of millions for a millennium. Creativity and electric initiative fairly light the air; yet, tradition and conservation rule.

Nice for me, I now hike a fresh trail, totally unknown to me for reasons other than my faulty memory.

By the bye, sorry, Astorga, maybe I'm biased, but I do believe Galician gals have you beat. In the interest of science, I'm prepared to repeat my observations however, and to reconsider my findings.

- - - - -

Finally found the hostel in Negreira. No way is it only 22 km from either the hostel or cathedral in Santiago. A more pleasant surprise (for someone who carried a chess set from Milano to Santiago), I've found a game at last!

8:30 a.m. to 5 p.m., Sat. 30/4/11,
From Negreira to God knows where

Well, I'm there, and still call it "God knows where." Oliviera, as the locals may name it, remains 35 km from Finisterre, close enough for me to finish tomorrow I hope. Nowhere nearer the finish promises an albergue. To reach here before 5:00 meant hard hiking, pushed again by another young German. When he and two friends, admittedly chasing me, suddenly appeared behind me, I broke into a gallop, which he matched, until I took the pace to a pack-bouncing, heart-stopping sprint.

His friends found this hilarious. Past Santiago, hikers are serious though. So they let the sole fool go.

At the albergue now, I enjoy a more restful pilgrim experience: listening to the best Spanish guitar music I have ever heard live—and on the oddest instrument. I'm forced to credit an eccentric Englishman for both. This fellow peregrino, returning from Finisterre, merely practices on his homemade collapsible instrument. As we part ways tomorrow, I'll never hear him perform again—the Brit bastard!

Yet another style of architecture (particularly in corn-cribs) appears created by crossing another ridge. Today's way appears remarkably isolating to me. Much of it slips through forest or empty farmland. You may feel quite alone, unless your friends sneak up behind you like ninjas.

May Day (Pope J.P. II beatified)

Oliviera to Finisterre? Less than two months from Italy, I reach The End of the Earth. Pushing sixty, I'm not yet pushing daisies. Whatever your age, carrying a pack across Italy + France + Spain, minus two months = hard goin'.

Amazing sights I've seen along the way, but the most amazing—and disappointing—Providence saves for the final day. Right in front of me, a taxi just dumped three "pilgrims" at the last roundabout before the last stretch of trail. What are these people thinking? Who do they try to kid? God? Little effort puts me past these pretenders.

Why? I guess I can understand folks who, jealous of other pilgrims, dishonestly acquire Compostelas. Can't these phonies leave at least Finisterre to real pilgrims? What are they thinking? How can we share a planet?

- - - - -

Just when I was setting the record for reaching Finisterre, bells tolled to remind a papist pilgrim of his Sunday duty. Unluckily tired legs stumbled into a confirmation service, with celebrant in full-throat at full-throttle. Attending Mass can inspire, but ingesting an hour of Spanish prattle can poison a soul. I nearly needed my stick to beat my feet into motion again, and no one remains now to chase or to chase me. This church did prominently present St. James and St. Roch to help me out of the door. I have granted permission for burial in Galicia, or anywhere "Irish" on the Camino, but my funeral must be in English, as I would not be caught dead in another Mass like that. I feel half dead now. Also, avoid planting me among eucalyptus. Good luck.

One final stone ceremony I performed prior to Finisterre, after two dogs flew at me. No, I did not ritually stone the dogs or their pea-brained masters who chose the Camino to exercise leashless pets. My prayer-pile sought forgiveness for fools and mercy for their victims, even for the pseudo peregrinos in both categories.

- - - - -

Recovered from the shock of finding 3 km more to go after Finisterre, I dutifully continued to the famous lighthouse long before sunset, after settling into the municipal albergue. That "refusio" takes seriously their duty to document and accommodate true pilgrims only, God bless 'em.

Beyond the lighthouse I communed and communicated with compadres. Sharing my opinions, I sought theirs, employing three questions I'd asked myself after Santiago: 1) What did you most enjoy about your pilgrimage experience? 2) Like least? 3) What wisdom will you take away from the Camino? (Appendix I.)

Nearly noon, Mon. 2/5/11

Finisterre to Muxia. Sharing experience and wisdom with my newest friends (mentioned above), "The Three Amigos" (one Yank, two Gerrys), pleased most. In Finisterre I sought and bought Santiago tarte to share as well, but could not find my pilgrim pals who had all finished in Finisterre. "Pink Pants," the psycho who followed us from Oliviera, I spotted six times (possibly due to his pant's hue) but saw no sign of my amigos. I did not eat the whole treat myself but shared it with others (not penniless pink lunatics), further delaying my departure for Muxia (Moo-shia), an unknown destination before I nearly reached my previous final goal. Finisterre had come as news to me the first time I hiked to Santiago. Naturally the tourist office is now closed, as no printed guide points the way for me, and I have no one to follow. Few continue past Finisterre.

That means needing to bid adios to many casual acquaintances too, bound to me by surprisingly serious ties. Breaking these bonds hurts, because they're unlikely ever to reconnect. Worn soles drag my heavy soul on an even lonelier march than to Finisterre. The way feels more surreal, even though the most real part of the Camino stretches to Muxia. Here no distraction mars meditation. No bars offer libations every 50 feet. Tiny hamlets dissected yield no word of English or interest in tourists. Yet, you finish in a town offering everything. Most importantly, two old churches grow from ancient rock. Here one can hear and see the sea, and the sea air invigorates my brain enough to find €100 I'd hidden too well, and to deliver for pilgrims the following wisdom. Start at 9 a.m. at the first and final albergues when doing St. Jean P. de P. to Finisterre, to fully enjoy good facilities there (plus picture perfect villages), and in destinations, Roncevaux and Muxia.

Setting out earlier should not be necessary.

By adjusting your starting time to 7 a.m. (in April), the same can be said of everywhere else on El Camino. Don't bother yourself, or others, by starting in the dark. Unenforced rules forbid stirring from bed before 6 a.m.

If you can't get with the schedule, consider private accommodation. That goes double if you're a champion chainsaw snorer. When you do wake the rest of us, please drop all annoying pretense of consideration.

If, due to inconsiderate actions of other, you do rise early, leave off the lights, including any on your head or hand. Gather belongings in two loads to carry outside, where you may putter and chatter amongst them to your heart's content, planning your Camino in detail ad nauseam.

Planning actually needed, for the 900 km march from St. Jean to Finisterre, amounts to: 30 km/day for thirty days. Do more some days to do less on other days whenever you like. Don't try to do it all in double-time.

Whether or not the course runs rough or smooth, up or down, hot or cold, anyone who can't turn out 30 km on any day has no business flying to France to prance over the Pyrenees. Want to walk slower than 5 km per hour? Walk longer than six hours per day. I've perambulated sixteen hour days regularly, repeatedly, and have finished as many as 80 km in a day. In April any day generally offers for play twelve hours of light.

Mid-April to May strikes me as the only time to commend doing the Camino Francais.

Faster trumps longer for most folks. Given an extra half hour for good measure, you can still deliver 10 km before a 9:30 breakfast; 10:00 to a 1:00 lunch burns another 10 km of calories and allows an extra hour for easing through the heat of the day; take three hours off to rest in the shade or air-conditioning, before letting 4 p.m. put you back on the path for a 6:00 finish of another decade of km. If you've dallied, go till 7:00. You still complete long before dark and full hostels. On a nice day in easy terrain, do double distance easily.

If you prefer to hike in the cool of the evening, you would still have a couple hours of light or twilight after 7:00 if you need or desire to find another hostel. Before leaving, ask the hospitalero to phone ahead.

All peregrinos should ever be prepared for finding no accommodation or pulling up lame far from help. That doesn't mean packing a tent or other heavy gear. Carrying pounds of survival gear can kill you. Remember you can mail 7 kilo for 7 euros anywhere in Spain, in order to have stuff wait for you in Santiago. You will need to reach there inside three weeks though. Don't let me catch you lugging a tent across Spain. The deal from the U.S. Post Office improves on Spain's for pilgrims on the Appalachian Trail.

Having battled from Italy, I feel qualified to give unqualified praise to Muxia, as yet unspoiled. Into Muxia I marched in timely fashion, in time to book into one of the better hostels on the Camino and still reach the pilgrims' office before closing, plus the seaside chapel before sunset. There I shared the last of six Santiago tarts.

Warning: the most expensive, most almondy tarts more likely contain more almond shells. Most sellers in Santiago can see you coming from 900 km away. Find the single supermarket downtown to pay half the usual price.

My record of passing all comers and none passing me I extended unintentionally into Muxia. No longer feeling any need to push myself, I would have allowed any good hiker to pass. No one appeared.

Tues. 3/5/11

Muxia to Santiago by bus. Finally, I can board a bus without carrying aboard the extra baggage of shame or guilt. Many days of hiking I now ride in hours, in comfort. Along with predictable relief, I also feel surprising regret.

Even the station restaurant in Santiago a poor pilgrim can frequent without guilt. This place serves a croissant on a plate with knife and fork, but still does not embarrass with the price. This station also provides a great selection of inexpensive buses to the airport—duly noted for tomorrow.

Wed. 4/5/11, Santiago to Stanstead, England

Man alive! Today's race nearly killed me. Climbing over hill and dale for 3,000 km, I forgot how demanding and unforgiving are "civilization's" sudden short hikes. My exit route I should have researched better, but I believed the folks paid to aid tourists when they told how easy I could exit by bus. My mistake. Fierce pressure, more than real exertion, soon had sweat pouring.

Finally found, the bus sat in traffic in the bus station, where every tick of the clock slapped my "clock." When bus doors shunted open at the airport, I sprang out like the cuckoo on a clock, with equal knowledge of where to go. Having only one chance (if any) to choose correctly, I hit hard the closest door as I heard my flight's final call. Seeing the security line for boarding, I did not see check-in or time/need to find it. Holding a computer generated boarding pass, I jumped at the first security gate.

This shortcut could have cut me later, were I less practiced in bluffing my way when traveling. It did cost immediately a fine hickory hiking stick. Though specifically cut to airline specifications, it could not escape the attention of security in an airport where most passengers arrive with sticks. To find check-in would not only cost me my flight and ticket, but also outrageous surcharges for carrying a short stick. Had I one minute to spare, I would have tried to bluff the guard, but with time and a queue pushing me, I yielded up my stick, though I would rather have sacrificed anything else, including a digit or two. Cursed spite!

My plane would be further delayed of course. Yet with all the time in the world, I could never have smuggled three bags into the cabin if I still carried a cudgel. Teddy Roosevelt's axiom doesn't apply. Sometimes you better not talk at all or carry any stick.

My pilgrimage complete, I share an axiom of my own with all who might share The Way someday. I believe Ye Olde Camino de Santiago had much to teach the upstart Appalachian Trail; but while the former remains more rational, the latter offers a basic truth.

If everyone who visited Baxter Park in Maine, the final stretch of the A.T., claimed to have "finished the A.T.," while technically correct, they would not walk with Christ, the truth that sets you free. Yuh, I know peregrinos are supposed to accept all comers, but should not all hikers shame the devil, call a lie a lie? Should not the Catholic Church discourage falsehood and relativism? Section-hikers and day-hikers should not be called thru-hikers or peregrinos, or granted dedicated facilities, because that would support a lie, make a mockery of pilgrimage.

If unable to cross more than the cathedral square, you may yet consider yourself a pilgrim, but don't say to me or others, "I'm a pilgrim of St. James" (and write a book!), if you have not attempted even to cross a provincial border, or one mountain, for He who climbed Calvary for you.

APPENDIX I
Survey of Pilgrims

1) **What did you enjoy most about your pilgrimage experience?**
2) **Like least?**
3) **What lesson did you learn?**

1) Santo Domingo: saint, cathedral, albergue, and town. Here's the paradigm for all the Camino.
2) Disliked pseudo peregrinos clogging the Camino and albergues in the later stages.
3) Though not God, I can do miraculous things if I but ask God, and I will ask.

[The Mad Quick Mick]

1) Enjoyed the variety of the Camino, how all fits together into one whole, which was never as scary as feared.
2) Disliked fears she (a teenage girl) had brought to the Way, due to scaremongering by folk who'd never done it.
3) Don't fear to do, even to fail, due to doubts of others especially if they couldn't know what they're talking about.

[Fearless Frieda, German teenager]

1) Enjoyed meeting and conversing with so many different types of people, who share so much, but also enjoyed silences, sometimes when alone, sometimes with others.
2) Larrasoana Albergue (16 km short of Pamplona). Filthy!
3) Going home even more open to other people and ideas, and less worried about timekeeping and all the details of living unessential to life. Intend to travel more and worry less about it.

[Laughing Peregrino, German man, 30s]

1) Liked the experience of walking in solitude, over long distances, day after day.
2) Disliked the commercialization of the Camino, the touristy peregrinos.
3) Doesn't know yet what she's taking home, as she isn't home yet.

[Dutch Greta Garbo, 50ish]

1) Simplicity of living. Knowing what you'll be doing every day, even though every day is different, unexpected.
2) Lack of consideration from fellow peregrinos, who just don't seem to know better. Society is socializing poorly.
3) Knowledge taken from the Camino is very personal, about life and love with someone.

[Male Dane, 25ish]

1) Just being alone with friends (which did not include this author).
2) Did not care for the final 100 km crowded with tourists.
3) Don't know yet.

[German woman, 30]

1) Fellowship. Meeting the whole world, discovering how much we differ, and yet remain the same, because the personal challenges we face remain very similar everywhere in the world, but especially on the Camino.
2) Did not like bedbugs. (As a trained medic, he treated people with bad bites.)
3) His faith in humanity restored, including him. Intends more involvement in his Catholic parish's pastoral work.

[American man, 40s]

1) Freedom and independence, of movement and action, the opposite of what "pilgrimage" suggests to the uninitiated.
2) Commercialization.
3) Will be more open with strangers and foreigners at home.

[German man, 25?]

1) Meeting people.
2) Rubbish, litter, worse, in albergues and along route.
3) No time to consider, as she rushed to meet someone.

[German woman, 25?]

1) The sincerity of fellowship. The usual social questions actually seek real answers here.
2) Snoring.
3) Determined to be more considerate and genuinely helpful at home.

[English woman, 45]

1) Every day different.
2) Not knowing what was happening, on the Camino or in the outside world.
3) Will research more in future before heading off somewhere half-cocked.

[Englishman, 50]

Admitting only hiking from Sarria, three German women disqualified themselves from speaking about pilgrimage. God bless 'em.

[The three Sorry Sarria Sisters, 30s]

1) Flowers, moss, nature's perfume.
2) Blisters.
3) The knowledge of their capability to do big things if they just set their minds to it.
1) The same.
2) Rain.
3) Agreed.

[two young ladies from Germany]

1) Portable solitude.
2) The Portugal Route's use of roads, frequented by dangerous Portuguese drivers.
3) Learned to be more patient, in heart and mind.

[Middle-aged American woman]

1) Nature in springtime.
2) But spring rain near Santiago spoiled arrival, dampened spirits, and made more irritating the cathedral crowds.
3) Taking time to consider what's really important.

[German man, 60s]

One woman answered questions by questioning. She did not accept not liking some part of the Camino, as even pain and suffering form an essential ingredient of the whole. True. Here's where the reasoning of budding Buddhists fails. Acknowledging the goodness of the experience, even unpleasant parts, means accepting that counter-Camino forces, even pleasant ones, are bad. Our needing Bad to appreciate Good may mean some good resides in anything, but that doesn't mean Bad is Good, or is justified.

["Euro-girl," 20s, probably S. African]

One young man considered himself unable to answer even though he had walked from Marseille to Muxia. As he intended to walk home, he considered his Camino only half complete. He did know he disliked dealing with "tourist pilgrims" though. He immediately conditioned his comment by adding, "We must accept them." Why?

[Frenchman, 20s]

Another young man came on Camino in order not to think. He asked no questions beforehand, and refused to ask any afterwards.

[Slovenian, 25ish]

1) The variety of scenery, terrain and weather.
2) Rude people, especially those who continually rise before 5:00 a.m.
3) Appreciation for the cosmopolitan atmosphere of El Camino; the experience of meeting a wide variety of strangers and being able to talk with them because of one experience all had decided to share.

[Swede gent, 65]

1) Most impressed by the smiles and tears of other pilgrims on reaching Santiago.
2) Was not bothered by anything other than the Camino ending.
3) Did not feel his English sufficient to answer such a serious question.

[Frenchman, 50s]

1) Communing with nature.
2) Nothing upset her, not even blisters, as she learned to endure, and to overcome.
3) Surprise: she is physically capable of far more than she thought; pain can be surmounted spiritually; discovering (as a Protestant) that "Holy Places" do exist, where God is easier to find.

[Finnish woman, 50ish]

1) Discovering about herself, especially her feeling so at home.
2) Discovering the Way so crowded after Leon.
3) Herself.

[Austrian woman, 25ish]

1) Being able to listen to his heart, or to God, when walking alone.
2) Pilgrim partiers, and being treated like one by hospitaleros in the later stages of the Camino.
3) A new self returns to Korea to discard the old.

[Korean man, 22]

A middle-aged German couple were just totally grossed out by the piles of shite and paper left all along the Way.

[German couple]

1) The wide variety of good food to be found.

2) Pilgrims failing to appreciate El Camino, from failure to put more into it. Recommends repeating the Camino.

3) Rewarded by Spain (particularly hams and cheeses).

[Elderly German, 12-tour veteran]

1) Forest paths.

2) Murderously disliked roosters crowing at dawn.

3) Have learned what's important, really needed.

1) Ditto.

2) Nothing.

3)Consumer culture is crap.

[young Estonian/Spanish couple]

1) Time to learn about oneself, in action.

2) Terrorista tourista para-greenos; being treated like one.

3) Her true self.

[Hungarian woman]

1) The quietness of El Camino Primitivo, after accepting the entire Camino Francais has become a giant tourist trap.

2) Nothing, as even the disturbing cities made him appreciate more the quiet countryside.

3) Confidence in his own vision for himself.

[Young Italian man]

1) Friendliness of folks living and working along the Way.

2) Uncheerfulness in peregrinos, grimness in pilgrims.

3) Can carry back to school, to classroom and playing field, the memory of greater weariness than he'd ever known, and the confidence that he could carry on and achieve.

[Italian youth]

1) Time to think about life and his true nature in nature.
2) Others snoring, and his walking when short on sleep.
3) New eyes with which to view life.

[Another Italian youth]

1) Walking with friends.
2) Sleeping in large, crowded dorms.
3) Feeling God will grant more years of good health.

[Middle-aged German man]

1) Kindly people on Camino and living along it.
2) Commercialization of Camino.
3) Deflated by finally arriving, he waits to see what comes.

[Ditto]

1) Overcoming sore feet, while walking through bountiful nature.
2) Sore feet.
3) Will be more observant and calm while walking through life in future.

[Finnish 50ish couple, totally in tune]

1) Nature.
2) Pontferrada albergue. Too big. [I was lucky there, as arriving late meant a huge dorm for just a few overflows.]
3) To always smile when meeting strangers in future.

[Mexican, 24]

1) Meeting people.
2) Meeting tour-bus pilgrims.
3) Learning not to rush. Will slow down and enjoy life more.

[Young Spanish woman]

1) Meeting above young Spanish woman (very pretty).
2) Disliked his old self, previous thinking and values.
3) Starting the Way in a hurry, he learned to slow down once he met the girl. Duh.

[Young Spaniard]

1) Small, friendly albergues on the Camino Primitivo.
2) Rude pseudo peregrinos on the Camino Francais this couple called "Trampas" (cheater in Spanish).
3) Friends.

[An Aussie couple in accord]

1) Meeting folks from all around the world, all sharing a common purpose.
2) Walking with pain.
3) Learning how much pain can be endured.

[?]

1) Quiet.
2) Mud.
3) Peace

[American woman]

Peace came from suffering with other pilgrim souls, not just from all around the world, but from the past.

APPENDIX II
Hostel Towns on El Camino

This schedule completes El Camino in one month, from France. For a side-trip, sick-day, or continuing to Muxia, save a day, any day, by doing a double-hike or trading-in one of three extra days allowed. *Buen camino!*

Bold type suggests **day hikes**, * a reason to stop tonight

Refuge	Km.	Rating
Roncevaux	27 hard	****
Zubiri	15	**
Larrasoana	5.5 bad	-
Arre Villava	12.5	
Pamplona	3	***
Cizur Minor	5	**
Zariquiegui	6	
Uterga	6	
Obanos	4.5	**
Puente La Reina	2.3	***
Cirauqui	7.5	**
Lorca	5.5	**

Villatuerta	5	
Estella	5	**
Ayegui	2.7	
Villamajor de Monjardin	7.3	***
Los Arcos	12.5	***
Sansol	7	*
Torres del Rio	1	**
Viana	11	***
Logrona	9.5	***
Navarrette	13	***
Najera	16	****
Azofra	6	
Ciruena	9 bad	
Santo Domingo	6	****
Granon	6.5	*
Redecilla	4	**
Viloria de Rioja	4.5	
Villamayor del Rio	3.5	
Belorado	4.7	***
Tosantos	5	
Villambistia	2	
Espinosa	1.5	
Villafranca Montes	3.7	***
San Juan de Ortega	12 hard	**
Ages	3.7	
Atapuerca	2.5	

Burgos x **2 days**	21.5 bad	****
La Villalbilla	6.2	
Tardajos	3.5	
Rabe	2	
Hornillos	8.2	**
Hontanas	10.5	**
San Anton	6	*
Castrojeriz	3.7	***
Puente Fitero St.Nicholas	10	
Itero de la Vega	0.7	**
Boadilla del Camino	8	**
Fromista	6	**
Poblacion de Campa	4	
Villalcazar de Sirga	9.7	**
Carrion	6	***
Calzadilla de la Cueza	17 bad	*
Ledigos	6.2	
Terradillos de los Templarios	2.8	*
SanNicolas del Real Camino	6	*
Sahagun	5	**
Calzada del Coto	3	*
[Calzadilla de Hermanillos]	*alternative*	**
Bercianos	7.2	
El Burgo Ranero	2.8	
Reliegos de las Matas	13	**

Mansilla de las Mulas	6	***
Villarente	6	**
Arcahueja	5	
Leon (2 days)	9	****
Virgen del Camino	7.3	*
Valverde de la Virgen	4	
Villadangos	14.5	*
San Martino	4.3	*
Hospital de Orbigo	6.3	***
Astorga	16.5 hard	****
Murias de Rechivaldo	4	
Ste. Catalina	5	**
El Ganso	4.2 hard	*
Rabanal	7	***
Foncebadon	5.5	*
Manjarin	4.2	
El Acebo	7 hard	**
Riego	3.7	*
Malinaseca	4.7	***
Pontferrada	8	****
Cacabelos	15.5	**
Villafranca del Bierzo	7.2	****
Pereje	7.2	
Trabadelo	5	**
Portela de Valcarce	3.5	*
Vega de Valcarce	2.7	**
Ruitelan	2	

La Faba	5.5	
Laguna de Castilla	2.3 hard	
O'Cebreiro *Galicia!*	2.6 hard	***
Hospital de la Condesa	5.5	*
Fonfria	6.3	
Triacastela	8.7	
Calvor	12	
Sarria	12.5	***
Sarria (for a sorry-ass camino start)		***
Barbardelo	5.2	*
Ferreiros	8	**
Portomarin	8.6	***
Gonzar	7.7	*
Hospital de la Cruz	3.6	
Ventas de Naron	1.4	**
Ligonde	3.1	
Eirexe	1.3	
avant Palais	6.4	**
Palais del Rei	1	**
San Julian	3.2	**
Ponte Campana	1.3	*
Casanova Mato	1.3	
Melide (*primitivo* meets)	9.3	***
Ribadiso de Baixo	11	
Arzua	2.7	
Santa Irene	15.6	*

Arca O Pino	3.2	***
Monte do Gozo	16	
Entrée de Santiago	3.5	*
Santiago de Compostela	1 (*2 days*)	*****
Negreira or	22 (?)	**
Vilaserio (summer?)	12	
Oliveiro	33	*
Cee	18	
Finisterre	16	***

APPENDIX III
𝒯inis

June 2011

To the newlyweds,

Having hiked serendipitously from a wedding in Genoa, through the Maritime Alps, across all of France, over the Pyrenees, across all of Spain to Santiago and Finisterre, the End of the Earth, and having returned via Ireland in time for your wedding, I present to you the following fitting gift:

- The very first hard copy of the recounting of my hard pilgrimage, in which your wedding features.
- More durable than the hard copy, a piece of white Italian marble (carried over the entire journey) represents the difficulty and purity of my pilgrimage and of the one on which you now embark.
- A perfect match of this stone I left at the altar of St. James, sacred subject of my quest, in Santiago Cathedral—the holy goal of millions for 1,000 years.
- That rock remains there, as an offering for prayers from the patron of pilgrims, to join with mine for you. "*Adelante! Por Dios y Santiago!*" May you always walk with Christ.

- As tradition now demands, I return with a pilgrim's staff for family newlyweds. Unable to bring my faithful companion from El Camino (deprived me at the airport), I substitute one from our family farm, one that has helped me over the hills from home and back. Let it remind two travelers of home.
- For the distaff, a special pilgrim bowl I bring. May it always be full (except when collapsed for carrying).
- A pane of antique pressed glass, manufactured where the groom's folks grew up...
- also provides for the bride: something old (new to her), and something blue, and borrowed too, in a manner of speaking. May it be the only pain received today.
- To aid you on your way, to prevent pain, and possibly to save your lives, accept Avon's Skin-So-Soft, which (I just learned) U.S. Marines employ to ward off ticks, fleas, midges and mosquitos.
- A pilgrim's mini-Bible completes the set, brought from the Appalachian Trail to complete El Camino.

P.S.: Good luck on your journey. Your luck (blessing) has already begun, as rain held up for your preferred nuptials in a hayfield, and I managed to stifle a sneezing fit precisely during your vows. Hope you appreciate that present.

Buen camino!

Buen Camino!
May God aid
all pilgrims &
all who help
pilgrims!
El Peregrino
de Santiago
The Mad Quick Mick